Mar 19
IREF
2c
1/31/19
U=9

Anansi

DONATION

sunfall

sunfall

NEW AND SELECTED POEMS
1980–1996

Dennis Cooley

163318

Published in 1996 by
House of Anansi Press Limited
1800 Steeles Avenue West, Concord, ON
Canada L4K 2P3

Distributed in Canada by
General Distribution Services Inc.
30 Lesmill Road
Toronto, Canada M3B 2T6
Tel. (416) 445-3333
Fax (416) 445-5967
e-mail: Customer.Service@ccmailgw.genpub.com

Distributed in the United States by
General Distribution Services Inc.
85 River Rock Drive, Suite 202
Buffalo, New York 14207
Toll free 1-800-805-1083
Fax (416) 445-5967
e-mail: Customer.Service@ccmailgw.genpub.com

CATALOGING IN PUBLICATION DATA
Cooley, Dennis, 1944–
Sunfall
ISBN 0-88784-580-0
I. Title.
PS8555.O65S86 1996   C811'.54   96-930633-4
PR9199.3.C66S86 1996

Cover design: Pekoe Jones/Multiphrenia
Printed and bound in Canada
Typesetting: ECW Type & Art

House of Anansi Press gratefully acknowledges the support
of the Canada Council and the Ontario Arts Council
in the development of writing and publishing in Canada.

For Diane

Contents

4

hurtin song

                a crack of wind &
                    whack
                            the leaves
        fall off
                in a fit of electricity

they shiver all over the sidewalk
those fat little tongues ripped from shoes

this is not paris it is the prairies
aviaries the air at dawn falls from
the most brilliant stars anywhere

& the sun shrills till you cannot tell
is it the grasshoppers or the sun or telephone wires
the long grass the dust the wheels revolving

the lightning drains electricity from our bodies
        this happens every summer

& what is there left
                snow that falls like dandruff
                the solace of shoelaces

our hearts still rattle like lightning rods

I

1980–1995

From *Leaving*

Jan / us

        angered with you
          I read
  alone in the lamp
    light late
into a January night
      pressing through
  words that do not hold
    pages that will not hold
       my eye
   across
    the same passages
  again and a
    gain wanting
 to be taken
   in by the black
 shapes
   the clean blank spaces.

the house
    snaps and gives
     in the tightening
  cold exhales its stale
 breath draws the heat
   into the wind
      pumping black/
          white
     outside
  the window.

       limp
        I lock the door
    climb
      the steps to bed
 undress
    in the cool
     room

listen to your
                    too even
                    breathing
          in and out
beneath the light
                    down comforter
and in the
          dark / your eyes /
                    I see
          are glistening
    wet.

From *Fielding*

IV

Friday morning
(Feb 23)
in your down-filled parka
lined boots softened to your foot's shape
the house emptying now
relatives gone
Diane and the girls gone
Sharon & Laurel leaving soon
mom in tears
someone else cut out of her house
you could write sometimes

all the letters i never wrote
listen Irene, Irene, if anybody needs a bed
i have a big room, yes

Pat's car rolls east to Winnipeg
300 miles
windows clear   returning
coarse snowflakes
slope across road
slow roil   sun/hole
punched in
aluminum sky

in my dream
/one winter/
we were dreaming
you & i

cattails
broken back
on themselves
clumps of fireweed rusting thru

7

                    clover
                 almost oily
                              glows
             & ridges in banks fluting
                                   down & in
                     on themselves
stress lines
                   lesions in a giant brain
wooden wind
                   breaks along north side

                        sloughs clogged with reeds like
                                    broken sticks

pass an oil well
             deformed birdhead
                     pecking at the crude oil
   gushing spasmodically up from the casing
  oncoming grader
                        blade scrapes the shoulder
                   & snow peels off
                              clouding
another well chopping   slower shorter strokes
                   and straggles of trees
                                   hang black
                   onto the low spots
           bunch & we move east
                         trunks strangled with winter
                                  priming now with
                                          light
              stand in strange
                         relief against the sky
                   no depth   total depth
no this is

              not what i wanted
                         to say nothing i should be writing

     road   bare   sun
                                 sands ice away

more wells   they voted conservative here
                Diane's mom on the short wave
                      hoarse in her chest & throat
                      can't make out what
                                        she's saying
                                  the car's shadow
                                              running
                                     steadily
                                              beside us

            beside ourselves
snowdrift stalling behind

turbulence decreases with viscosity, as the measure of the
internal function of the stream, the ability of the stream
to stick together, to withstand shear.

hit the abrupt
                      drop into the valley
                        ice & snow
                                built up
            Pat rides the ruts worn into the highway
                        like a crosscountry ski course
                ravine at bottom
                              ragged with brush
                    Moose Mountain Creek
                        a stiff black twist
      a sliver of land
          pitted with trucks &
                              halftons
ripping by with snowmobiles in the backs
                silver fuel tanks

                                  Rosco bins

          bound side by side
      hard scars in the snow
                    only the rush & rap of wind
            one thing you can always count on
                        in this country   Gordon said when we
            looked for the graveside on the hill north of town
                                      the thrum of car eating
                                  fossil fire

what is the use of talking

        ruined yards & barns
)our yellow brick house that burnt down
      after we left the farm(
             & they have broken my house

2 brown horses
      feeding on bales
   in one corner of a pasture
           shaggy winter coats
)soft muzzles
              water snorting
      ice on long hair

)& the cows
               their breaths
     stifflegged run
     the frozen trough
     puffing jets of vapour
        orange cat her back warm
   & tea-bag smell of hay
     breathing into barn
        sweet breath
squashed one night flat in the stall
      frost growing out of the nails

a true statement from our records

not empty this space is not empty
          where is the poem in this
          locked in this
                calm

                                     & earth turns

       under us

#18 east &

           houses knotting regularly
                   every 7 or 8 miles
                   elevators like columns of dried blood
      snaring
                     names / numbers
        Bienfait Steelman Hirsch Frobisher Oxbow
Glen Ewen   Carnduff   Carievale   Gainsborough

         wires   tracks   roads
           twining
                 our doubtful lives over
                    this stunning plain

Oxbow
         Ralph Allen Memorial Museum
                     a converted railway station
    2 pigeons slap
            fast   from the side of the road
          595   the red metal stencil reads in the ditch
           at Glen Ewen a homemade sign
               YE   MUST   BE   BORN   AGAIN
                 red letters

the black railline tracks
                 us on the right
    telephone posts trail
               /pencils/
                   on the other side
       virgules that measure
             our passing
    sinking to periods
        out of sight
             their brittle braille
    stipples the prairie

wires that hum &
       sigh in the heat &
              the cold
& loudly shed the wind in storm

Carnduff
      Dale's hometown
        ice puttied on the road

Carievale 12 km
    highway a gash
             sometimes black / sometimes brown
       in the fresh snow
         barbwire fences
              splicing them with pliers
                in spring
      cracked dry
   stitching
     the endless seam between
               earth & sky
    bright white bleeding to
             uncertain white
      sky packed granular like
           crushed salt
            dissolving
      strong whiff of the coffee i drink/
          you drank/
     splashing in our nostrils
your death   turning
         father in
           my head / this poem
    Bob saying we silence words by
       writing them down
        from our records
sharp scent of your cigarettes in the parka i wear
im sorry to hear about your father dennis
    saltsour sweat i always liked
             wet in
shift   cramped in the seats

where we are strapped
windslap against car
billions of   new flakes   ground
off   sun

eyes hurt
in the reflection
frost folded   fibrous
in the air
grains of light
fogging the sky

but where are you my father
what trace of you in this
country you farmed & dug
this dirt
the wind erases

inside glass feel warm
yellow rub
against back of neck arm
barely awake
nap over the drowsing fields
& under crust
muffled grouse   crouch   hidden
in gauze pockets

will flash
when sun touches them
off
sun will wipe
off dazzle
so March inks in
like broken veins
raw scraggle of crows
coalblue bruises
on wet snow
aaaaaawwwwww   **aaw**
damp earthsmell
April scrawl of frogs

                                        slippery green
days drawn darkly thru
                    smother of frost
                            that he eat of the barley corn
                            and move with the seed's breath

                    now there is only
                the freeze of wind
            sawing the drifts
opening furrows
                        inside our
                            dozing
                    wind & a
                            blunt sun

& we are skinbags of heated water   dreaming
                            brains greyly
                balloon in our heads
                                nerves skein   blind
                                albino seaweed blown
                        our bodies' pools
                                        listening

                    carbon phases / your phrases
                                strung between us father
                        your breath tumbles
                                        shining quiet
                inside my ribs
find your hand hard in mine
            your lines wound in
                            the stretch of my muscles
        still living
                        but you are dead
& we float like lost birds
                                    over this frozen
                    land reading
                            these things
                            that we know
                    the long silence slanting past
                                now in the mind

riding

    edges of sound

        simply past metaphor

sun   wind   snow   sky

    these lines/

        letters/

my words for i loved you

        thinking of you

David saying

    it is always better to be alive

From *Bloody Jack*

in his tangerine skin

we buried him
in mint condition
on his eyes
two georges
they shone like hens eyes
he inhaled the dark
hhhhgg hhggg
engorged it
like a badger breathing
for blood

when we shovelled him in
christ he was a gorgeous man
the eyes were breathing
& shining blood

in the park

Saw him again, today. At the Hjartarson Cafe. And forgot
my purse and had to go back next day and get it. Thank
god she wasn't there. Ran into him in the park by
Probert's place. I was strolling the baby like I have all
summer. In my new lawn dress this time. And such a fine
day. Sunshine freckling onto the ground smell of cut grass
and the sprinklers throwing spindles of light up into the
air. Sun like brandy and the orioles and robins all excited.
And I was thinking of him, then, the last time we met, him
and me. Clouds of mosquitoes at the fair and I find him
near the freak tent peeking hurryhurryhurry steprightup
folks at all the passer-bys out of the corner of his eye. But
Danny's messed his pants and he gets cranky so I take
him to the room there in the park. So hot then I think
maybe I will have a lemonade. Mrs Horner, lady from the
flat next door, says sure she'll look after the baby for
awhile I should just go and have some fun my hands so
full all the time, for a change. So away I go for lemonade.

Well, who should pop up just then when I'm lined up? But
there he is that same laughing in his eyes like everything
is funny only he likes it too. And I am so nervous all a
sudden I can hardly look at him so excited to see him I
must be shaking so bad everyone can see and he with
those eyes and his smile my god I feel like when I patted
that horse that time at the fair or something way I am so
ascared and so quick. And the sun keeps on running
rainbows in the sprinklers and those eyes. He says sure
come on lets get a drink and me so scared but why not
when do I see him and Danny's fine Mrs Horner said
don't worry and so I can hardly catch my breath that
sounds like a good idea.

Streetcar to the cafe way cross town and me sitting beside
him all the way laughing and talking. And he all the time
so close I can smell him. I can touch him, John. Hardly
knowing if I'll get back in time. Or caring. Don't worry.
Same thing at the cafe. Can't think of what I want and he
asks for two lemonades. And all I can think is him and me
there and the waitress watching but who cares and oh my
John I wish I could I wish we could and do you really if
my stretch marks and those others so young and oh my
body starting to sag like his balloon do you John do you
really if with your eyes the sad in them too and your black
hair and life in you like an orange would you then even
then would you would you

breaking up is hard to do

        looklook   hes break
                        ing the line
      2 feet from the end

    he just broke
      a word in two
    did you see that boy
      he must be
  strong
        flexible too the way he just up and
           bends at those joints
                lotta people cant even touch their toes
but hes so articu
          late
    ly stringing a line

my god she sd
my god sd she he must be
      writing a big book
        this time
          am not sd he

                  no hes not hes gonna fall
                & break his neck/ the fool
                sd Ann if he doesn't

    stop this fooling a
        (round)
          if he doesn't
      watch his
            step

gypsophila

                                                    now
                            the new snow brightens
                my window deepens
                                        lays it light
upon the ground
                    the grass below
                            that holds it gasgreen
                into the yellow warmth
                                    in early November
                    seeds tighten/flare
                        under this skin of
                            snow singing
                a billion glass suns
                        in the night
)   remembering
            Penny Lyn
                    her gypsophila
                                in our garden
                    puffs of gypsophila
                                    white vapour
                                        blown
                        around the orange
                    burn of marigolds

when in August the ochre
ate its way
scalding thru the
window of my room
& you bathd/breathd in
the slick white acid
inside untoucht
that moment
cool & still
inside the bed

                                        here
                in the mellow spill
                            of sunfall

            the wax spaces
                        tell me
you are gone
Nov 8
            your letter says
                        Toronto
            out of the tinbarn box clicks
) the winter dreaming
                  at my door
            the words that have not come
                        dont take my words love lightly
                  your voice tells
                                    the quick
      cells rising
                  flicker
      cells your body carries
                        growing
                              dividing &
                                    growing
                  growing & dividing
us now
you now
            these 2000 miles
                        a child's breath away

his muse in the guise of a loonie lady comes to him (& desire full in her face)

pudgy moon
              stuffed with sausages
              and sauerkraut
        nudges
you awake and
              cuddles on your pillow
there she is
              wide-eyed & glowing
thats her
              faintly puffing
              & smelling of beer
this crazy woman
she has climbed through the window
              when
(a) your back was turned
(b) she found the ladder
(c) you left it unlatched
(d) your lips are sealed
    you aren't talking, not a word of a lie
shes shoved
              the curtains aside &
there she is now
              rolling her eyes at you
i dont know
              whats got into her
but she seems to have taken a
              shine to me
        the dizzy dame
so she throws her hair
              across my face
then nuzzles my neck
        and wetlips my ear

        & she so pleased
              moving down over you
        so importunate
        she wont let you go

how unfortunate
back to sleep
she beaming & beaming
with love at you

the end of the line

reached out to send you this line

    out to send you this line reached

      to send you this line reached out

        send you this line reached out to

          you this line reached out to send

            this line reached out to send you

              line reached out to send you this

of the handbones lady

               & the stretch in my hand
          my hand stretching
      your breast as it turns
          firms
              & the brown forms
                   in my mouth
        fingers tongue raspberry seeds twist &
                your rolling &
your reach
        the skinsoft on hard
              quick swallow
                  breathing
         hot
       under cotton
          damp &
                  soft
   parting &
     falling
          the rising
cat orangeing off bed
     your feet the rough on the
           bottom dirty
      & you slip we
             slippery where
       by the light
            in the air
    still in our skin
          sunsmell
   moving
      sunslipping
        like frog
  light across
       fine hair swoop in your back
          is there your
    hand it is bones is a bone
    is touch & is rub
your knuckles
   my lady

                    of the handbones lady
                  ragweed oil in your wrists
                    nipple warm
        nipple hard

              over me
                softblood

                              eggwet
            slipping   hard
                  slow

                              in &

  we're in   & in   & in
                          & in   to

                    you over me
                          your eyes grey/green
              they are/

                          opening
          & the dark
            the dark flows in
                          into them
    you &   a door slams downstairs
  & outside   ttcchh   ttccchh   ttcchh
  the sprinkler needles red into tomatoes
                    & winds sudden
          shiver thru window
    beer bottles
            smooth
                cold breath
                on the porch
              & our   hold &   holding the
                                    smooth wet
              sweatsmooth
                  & rounding is
                              warming &
                        your boneturning
                that/i feel
                              once again
                  inside

                you & you
                        stagger in
grey
        eyes these eyes
                        your swollen low in throat our shake
            warm
                    (grey/
                            racing(
            it is diesling your heart/
                        it is a
                                tractor running &
                    running
            & we're running
                            & running
        spinning with the sun
                running & raining
                            wet pain in our mouth
            shaking us
                under
                        & over
        & over
                &
                all over
again

"Patrol Lights Flashed as I Ran from Police Station" Says Krafchenko

stars asizzle
acetylene   nuzzles thru steel
night
matted with fear

      stars are neurons thrown
           overboard

blabber of air   cold

      down that wall
as if i were a kite tail
           in may

light sprawls   from rectangle
        as i fall
  falls on me
crushes me   so i
my back my back

so i   pop
  on the sidewalk

      am a mucilage of crow
      smeared on pavement

my legs   the road

     a dog somewhere
          shouting
      shutup shutup for chrissake
  sticks of fear

insides threatening
to bust their suits of tissue

     hurry hurry hurry

drowning in air

     as i go vertebrae
     of boxcars shuddering to life
         lights cruise somewhere
         behind my eyes as i run
fire in my heel
my hands on fire

   moon a tin of carbolic salve

day hardens

till its stuck & then
stiffens to toffee

night slouches in & the dark
the dark flows in

& begins
to grow/ glow in yr fingers
what do you see
moon an ice cube
floating in rum
& the moon slippery
in her mouth
a cinnamon candy once

the thots clog up
behind eyeskin
as if they were
breaks filling up with blood
or dogs/ shaken

dont take my love lightly

so you listen to the night
cars wriggle past in worms of light
stars stare at you
they are beads helixing time
)   that night penny with the choker
on her neck
ohh   ohhh
the stars on her neck   then
warm from her body

just now
the wind shivers &
you can overhear
electric crackings in
blue tissues

                              a cap
              crinkling   over
              head

                         then blind
sloughing the last skin of night
        peeling it off
                    like her dress
        the chest of skin breathing
                    hard
                              hhaa haa
                    when they slide
              2 x 4 s of sun
                    inside my cell

              morning gulping
              bottles of night

              wet pain in our mouth
                              & the sky
                    coughing blood

i see them sawing

rumble of stacking

the sweet smell
new lumber in the sun
its smells let out
when the sawing is done to them
& the once in a while high sound
where the wood fights back
there is the sap running
out where they give the cuts
the men bending
over in a strange geometry of need
the veins sliced open stream with resin
    sharp odour in the afternoon sun
the shadow   strangely slows
when the pain drains out of the wood

    roots   branches   leaves

they finish it off with nails
a dead frame they nail together
they put me on to
morrow a dying body on a drying rack
billions of lives spasms held
by their sentence

the men in their long robes
who set up there
putting me on
it

my deerest Join,

they said you have lost
the court appeal and know, there is no more chance
for you, at all my love they say weel be
a lone the kids and me, i read about it
in the papers garie you remember him tos!
on the portsh this morning and i could onely glance
at what they sad i just can't see
what they ment when they sed it fit
the crime. that may be right for them Join
but its coled in bed at night and Dnns
kin asking for you to and once I dremt
how you wuld tutsch me close and we wuld roll on
the bed war warm and all over your hands
and your eyes your eyes my love but i was onti
when i woke up it was so cold + Im shousing your name
end i shall never forget you my love.

as always
your jipsy lady

Flanicia
xoxoxo

your dad is feeling
kind of
bad

by the red

by the red river
river so low
walk by the willows
feel the rains blow

feel the slow rains dear
feel the rains flow
september mornin
cold rain like snow

if you cant call now
call when you can
warm in your voice love
glad in your hands

you at my window
you at my door
hold me once more dear
hold me once more

leave you a letter
leave you this song
leave you my love dear
sayin so long

send me some words though
though they are numb
words to remember
when they will come

willows of green leaves
sprinklers of sun
spindles of air love
whiskey of sun

crow in a door dear
crow in a door
hungry for somethin
wont see you no more

so pay me no visit
pay me no heed
sun starts to rise
sun starts to bleed

headingly jail love
headingly jail
think of me penny
in headingly jail

by the red river
river so low
walk by the willows
blowin in snow

From *Soul Searching*

body parts

yeahyeahyeah   back there   i dunno
way back there somewheres

you mean you dont know
it was apparent he didnt & so
look i ain gonna wait on yuh hand & foot
we rummaged our way through
the place was a graveyard of salvaged parts
hed saved almost everything

we had to be careful not to step
on the eyes there were bags
& bags of eyes right by the counter
           staring at us   like beheaded people
& some of them had got squished

we found a cart
Mike & Gabe & Zeke & me
& we got started
   wasnt easy without help &
we hadnt done anything
like this before but we started heaving

toes patellas posterior vena cava ankles arteries
nerves they had a lot of nerve stacks & stacks
of them & this partsman with a fistful
like spaghetti brains bins & bins of brain just
sitting on the shelf there stupid as walnuts or
magnetos with their wires crossed or gone
hay wire & bones bins & bins of bones all kinds of
them teeth a big collection of teeth (yellow)
that rattled like cotter pins or dominoes when
you shake to see them kidneys skull caps shaved
& shelved dusty as headlights in small
town garages cases of cheeks & chins it was all there

somewhere gall bladders stacked millions of them in
stock bladders vertebrae like garlic or
nuts on wire hoops down one aisle trays
   of girdles curving
         lines & lines of spines strung up
                           to cure at the end
intestines intentional i spose drooping   I like
from ceilings like indoor water slides
livers idle as Domtar chemical plants   this
on shut-down hair of all colours & coarseness
hormones they were spectacular cortisone
insulin throxine adrenaline testosterone
estriol estradiol estrone progesterone
                              part

            Im telling you
it was all there miraculous display
   cases of these greens
      & blues in crystal rows
               tinkling
         /the milk man in morning

                  we got a lot of that

      that & jaws there was a special on jaws
            so we got some
      extra
               but it was awful
            hard to get fresh muscle

we blushed when we hit the
      Venal Section   & rushed
right past fast as we could
go so we got those pieces pretty
mixed up   I am afraid
when we pushed them in alongside
   the long slide
            of pelvic girdles

how much blood
dunno 20 30 litres or so i guess
& we got that too Gabe dipped it
out of a cask into an empty pail
we picked up a lot of things
that way at Cosmic Wreckers
there where we stood
in pools under stomachs

in one room a bunch of guys
on a doo-hickie like in one
of those places they fix shoes with
were polishing knee caps
& tossing them easy as hub caps
shiny as shins into compartments

some others lazing round
in the back room they got
knuckles spilled all over the table
        one guy digs in his pocket & out comes
    just fistfuls of knuckles

we pick up just about every damn thing
but nowhere any skin glue no
warranty no customer service no
guarantees on parts or service
there werent even any air pumps
for the flat lungs we found
    stashed like hot water bottles under the rib cages

the guy in charge couldnt care less
            he had a monopoly he didnt have to

so we check through the register
gonna haf ta get yr own water buddy
& he Pete his name is Pete hes workin
        for The Man   crams all the stuff
into a big bag of skin

as we leave the gates bang shut
behind us & we see something shiny
with anger in the air waving
behind us & I get this sickening
feeling we arent going to pull this off
things arent going to work out somehow
somethings left out weve left
something behind   back there
where broken bodies are stripped
down & where hearts leak
all over the floor

we done our best since
then but you got

           youve got to forgive me

    i cant help wondering

         about all those hearts

amusement park

spirits were electric
          they could
    bop across gaps & wink jagged as bees
into wrinkles & tubes of flesh
          sick with their
flashing fast & slick as neon

for eons they would crackle
down to light up
     our lives   electrons pouring through
our headlights bright
               as cornea
on the blue ends of street lamps

    incarnate & neat as nuns they would chummy
up on the seat and drive us
     round & round &
around gay &
               clumsy bumper crazy
cars creaky with desire
          sparking   in the dark

so we would jostle & jounce
each other & the spirits would
giggle up & down the cables
    all night we hung foetally on
we would lurch & jerk & jiggle
flatfooted as old men in polka

     spirits maintained
themselves on the overhead
     juices coursing in
so they would flit & spit

all in all the spirits gave us
         a lot
   of static

it was shocking   the way
)right out of the blue
          the spirits would come & take us
for
     a ride
          they would drive us
                    crazy

the glass bead game I

they floated & shone
in the sun they sang
they rang like wine
glasses when you run
your finger round
& round the rim
                    in rings
god was blowing them out

)child with a horn
through a golden wand   or wound
bundles of angels tumbled clear
          artesian water from
every angle imaginable
                          their want

transparent as childrens eyes
molten as love when the stars
(big things were taking place)
               sang & rubbed
together in the warble of night

there was a lot of hubbub of walking
to & fro when someone put on
the music of the spheres
they swooned   in linen airs

oh they flung themselves round
good in the morning of god
giddy as beads of cod liver oil

souls blinked on in mercury
street lamps in lonely towns
blue as tv sets they were a touch
cold fickle as stars are on silver screens

                    the finest crystal
souls that bent   over the light blent blue

& green rivers of light   in Cristal d'arc

thin & chique as contact lenses
they fell unto the upturned
eyes of the royal hens
gone near-sighted with waiting
they wobble & wink as if they were
eye lids on chickens in those
Versailles music boxes

emprismed they bled
          from the face of god
fled streaming as if it were
                    a nosebleed

From *Perishable Light*

prairie vernacular

what they edited in fall
left footprints where (the land
parched) rocks had stood & thot

inside overshoes of winter
under buckles of bins & barns
boots of pig pens
seeds peeped beneath breath
hid in hides with stacks of bones
that slept & dreamt   cabbage & corn

all winter long under the pages
under snow & ice spring rehearsed
small creatures waited for march
to ransack their rooms

each spring they ruled the land
like foolscap those farmers
laconic as typewriters
scraped its face free
from the fat of winter
from the water marks
spring left in its pressing

& then there is a certain
slant of light thats pencil-
sharpened to a tightness   in the grass

& august men come to kneel
& read what is written there
thousands of grains at their finger
tips they poured into the earth
till it was green with noise

bent &   watched over them
        till   /combining in fall :
              : the first   : : stammer

:   rattling   in the hopper

                                   then:
                     the heavy pour

        till we were sunburnt
/with words/
              fluent with them

in the fullness of light   the fullness of time

consider how the brain resembles

the slough or maybe more the pot
                    hole at the end
of our lane where the ditch backed up
every spring because
there   was no culvert

& the water sat there
            a fat lady
on the porch paralyzed
by heat & rats

but what there really was
was this
                    grey scum
    all over the water & on it   walked
myriads of insect eyes & wings
they   : squirts of ink: shimmied
            & scrawled on some
madness of fever   all over that dirty skin
                    quicksilver bent   under their
passing

                                & then the mosquitoes
chimed up like gothic
                script   you might say
tensed on parchment   chimera
when the camera stills them

& I have thot a lot
    about that since
it seems to be a   big
metaphor for something deep
but it wasnt   really
anything more   than that

you want me to say   huge
pike wallowed savagely   suddenly
out of murk shoved their

ugly snouts into the light
& busted the thin skin like a balloon
or a failed safe you want
something deep & dark
& you are wondering
                    where it is
    when will it   appear
but there wasnt   there almost never is
a nasty jack clicking below

you want significance
you are wondering

            how did this poem   get published

but there was   only me   & my sisters
    & the 95° Estevansun
        lowering ourselves
            great
    — skysmooth as a babys bum —
                    fully (we were
    parched(into
                — to the chin —
    of cold)   muddyhole
            at the end of our lane

the taboo on saying what you dont

you know i wish
i could have said
its a bird look its a bird man
snagged in the tree & flailing
around with its beauty
full song full of pain

or failing that
  a banana   full of light
upon which the black jangles are
      glued like in one
of those parisian decoupages in paris
          only a lot livelier   & lovelier
                      a decolletage
) (o
              ne of those pairs
      of panties on the line blooming   ( )

on account of the trees
  are really twiggy &
black & it shines like its skin
is bursting with light & leaking
      where a comma has ripped
          open the bag of night

i wish i could say that
it is a sucker   nudging in mud
a dent in a civil war canteen
the thumb of a japanese wrestler
          god knows
i wish i cld

but i have been reading
(the french again)
& now i know
you cannot say

it grinned like a monkey in the tree
   sighed like a pickerel
      gone belly up   in an oil spill

you cant even say it
is   a foetus of light
            or not even
      the eye of an albino frog
                  frozen in winter

they wont even let you say
      looklook its a goose
               stuck in mud
         a goddamn snow goose singing
            & singing its silver
      goose song at my window
                  down

you cant say any of those things
            not any   more
                  you cant
         because a word spreads & slides
                  like cheez whiz
never lines up
   with the world (there but for l
   go i) & if they did
         how would we know
they werent/   lying
                     slippery as fish
         you cant lay a hand on them

in this age of indeterminacy
            one things sure

we got moon musings
                  man
but we never got the moon

                  *

         & i never forgot

49

what i was taught
or what i thot
i was taught
of the moon

death

is not

power lines going down
        ripped out veins bleeding
to death & turbines turning on
frantic as hearts of hanged men
when brains of bright cities
see all their electricity seep away
        & planets plummet
    & go out

2.

death is

when it begins to wear out
the wiring brittle as peppermint
sticks out and the pipes plug up
with mineral sediments & sadness
sticks like egg to plates

reading or dozing over a newspaper
it is alone in ovaltine & glasses

old people are young
people time has happened to

                the body is old
                the body is cold
                the body wont do
                    it wont do
                it will never do
                    what it is told

    eyes are frightened back
up faster than clogged toilets

3.

it is clay
pots & leaves
fallen off plants or
planks
you give cold tea to
it is still
life
life is   very
still

From *Dedications*

a poem for the other wise

                    they are every
            where i tell you every
thing wrong with us they
            wont   let   go
    of the line   wont   let you in
            sist on their margins
      of relief   be
lief to   let things wriggle
                    from them a kind
            of bad breath

delirium—L., madness < *delirare*, to rave, lit.,
to turn the furrow away in plowing < *de* —, from
+ *lira*, a line furrow

        they know   exactly
                where   to draw
        the line they insist upon

                        a strange sense of letters
                            :   she wishes
        you'd "stop   this playing
around"

                                this getting out
            of line   this being ir
                responsible foot
            loose &   fancy/free

            we shld hold
    our   breath as long as we can
            the dirty river   whats around us
                we close our eyes to

log our time

            the form & technique
obliterate the feeling
        and the thought

                        when the little things
                                    at night
            shine on the bank & in
                the water   at night
                            no one   lets
        up   not even then
                            no one lets   go
                                                lets you
            be
not Ann or the other Anne   they wont
            give you   a break
                            they   deploy
                their lines they are
                                not a
                mused   they will not be caught
        out of line

not George   or Doug
                            certainly
                not Mark or Susan
                            not Brenda
                                not even her
                when you
                    throw things in for good
        measure

                            they wont hesitate
            to step in
                    in their made
            to measure lines

                            they just keep
holding the line as long as they can long as they possibly can

                    hide in (met
                            a phor
                    the hard of hereing
        when herein they take their (proper) measures

                            & you are   pretty
                    broken up about it

a curse on a critic

behind yr powered perriwigs & wings riggedy
jiggedy you porker out on little pigs feet
how you jig & hop yr pork chops a round
on those bonestiff ideas that look a bit like legs
vindictive with blondness bristling with bindertwine emotions

smug as a burgher (you are
soul) slackassed with notions you drop emotions
slung from what should have been a backbone
a wallet of farts   you wallow of warts   ferret of fear
my finest   truffles all my arts all are trifled (jewel
by jowl) by yr rifle eyes   you & your sluice of reviews

all tarted up & champing yr tartered chompers   iggety
ig   id like to say   yr thin as silver-fish you eat
my words but no toe   nailed by your cloven smirks ill
have to settle for letting you looming large as lard lord
ing it over us know how much i admire   & jigjig   envy

you & the ooozy grace your expansive breadth your
pockmarked porkbarreled ex   pensive brain jigjug goes
your slopbucket soul   you & yr gluttinous yr gelatinous
mind pickled in the vinegar of what passes
in the prig that gristles between
yur nazi bloodpudding smiles
what passes for feeling
in that heart plugged with fat
what (you pizzle of poetry)   you hunchknuckle marrowmush pass
/for thot   fatuous with flatulence

now   in throatsquint & eyesqueal in that
tin y un n erv(in)g nerVou s itC h th Efain test
collapse when — unclogging of eyes — you vaguely
knackers knicked & no thing left   you have the knack
                (munchsnuffle read   : jawdrop :;
)in little()red eyes (dimly sur
mise in instinct of sphincter begin to know the sligh
      test pres sure of poetry right be
                            tween yur eyes

police informer

I got this leather jacket see
a black one   right
its like a cop jacket
only a little slicker I like to think
one a   those American ones I guess yd say
        you know   Hill Street Blues
look a lot like Billy donja think

so anyways I just got this jacket eh
& the women they like it man
            a lot
its really soft & a bit puffy
            a winter one eh
so the women all want to touch it like
        so thats   ok with me
                I don mind
they can do   all the touching they want

but one time   one of the women
she reaches across
like Im just talking to her right
were havin a coffee & she
reaches across & touches the shoulder
& she says   get this   she says

c'ni see yr night stick   huh
that's what she said
lemme see
yr night stick

ok

From *this only home*

Annie

thinking of you Annie
    earth there some
        where
a cuticle of light

        sun I like to think will
        manicure
            in morning
        earth moving you in sleep
        turning our capsule moving

        find only the blackest black
           I ever saw
        earth complete
        inked in all the brackets
          full & some
            thing sinks
        a racket you feel
        but do not hear

        utterly blank ,
          blink & it's
        still there
          silent as death it is
        colder than icicles
           in your hands Annie
        the bicycle we rode & a cut
        on the thumb earth has become
          numb maybe

        Annie older
      than everything in your heart
        & as young

        everything is written
      or nothing

in the dark we track
            the stars link them
)bracelets)
            until the stars
(stop

                :that's earth
                    that's you
                blocking the light
                            carbon
                paper I cannot read
                    or write
                home to you

kids

those summer nights
               your wife & kids
      thikk thik   bugs on screens

gluey bodies of children
sleep sticks them onto night
they click in pale petals

          call from their dreams
               thick with it, the heat

   earth inside its thin bubble
               , breathing
   so thin you gasp in terror

you lying on the ceiling
you touch the face of
               a sky
          tenderly
as you would a child
               horrified
as if you were a child
          you touch the face

gravity

have felt stars swarm my face
my heart swim in my hand have
heard what Newton said the greater
the mass the stronger the pull
the further the distance the less attraction

           know only i am in a stone
                 I am a stone
           a child swings round &
           round as a moon a child tugs
           from far away holds me here
                keeps my thoughts
           from swarming
                     from flying off

my daughter on the other end
the cord stronger than gravity
feel the cord how it vibrates,
           heart in my hand

thieves of darkness

what can I tell you of this darkness
that it is iron only we float through
Orion cold as glass they store gasses in
and you are sucked into them at a touch
your inner ear bewildered

that it is an onion we are ions inside
& track its rings faithful as bottle collectors
as jewellers with their tricks & music boxes
except we hear no music no smells

that it is a black sack
we have untied
& fallen in
to sun & moon & stars
birds some hunters bagged
that in it we are seamen
swim or swarm
stars semen eggs

birds whose eyes have been poked out
we sing to the dark call to the sun
rickets breaking out from our bones
brittle as bricks
our bones break out from want of sun
the splotches we have become
is it sunspots flare our skin

that it clicks or chills or warms
us to know we are seamen, or worms
on a dark dark sea
that spreads before & speeds

something slings the sun past

                  a hot rock
              in awful whizzes
monstrous marbles we marvel & shrink from

                          only we
cannot hear this
            is not Daedalus dead
            his flimsy racket broken
                          strings & all
                    the flames the rickety
                    wind sun blew by him
                    in his wax & feathers
he could be a yellow jacket in sun

              the terrible vertigo
              the green spinning
                  at the end the rocket's red glare

              we seek and make ourselves
              sick we are in the dark I am afraid
              this blue dream of wonder & sickness

what he sees

it should be may the trees filling
as if there were no tomorrow instead
it is the new year it is cold and well
I do it anyway, swing the wooden cylinder
sawing the air with it there
              can be no saving now
swivel the matched eye glasses, my neck

I spy out the secrets of God's Heaven
I spy with my little eye and
my god my god what I see
what is there how can this be
          can this be

the most beautiful and delightful sight I
          rub my eyes no
                    I cannot
      believe my eyes
                    have stars
            in my eyes there are spots
in my eyes and I nearly fall

                    stars—thousands of them, billions
                    billions and billions of tiny lights
                              no one could have seen
                                   ever before
                         who could have seen
                         who now can believe

      stagger from the eye-piece
            headful of stars look
all you have to do is look for yourselves
            look why don't you

and the moon its face lumpy as an old cow
          something sudden

something so electric I can hardly stand
so unfixed I see a stake I try to steady
          myself at it and Bruno at it
a stinking candle howling for what he saw
                                and said

Kepler

I am Johannes Kepler keeper of the numbers and the stars
born inside religious war and broken joints
and I have seen bodies cracked open on hate and hunger
my own aunt roasted alive at the stake and my mother
almost my wife burnt away on a fever in war
men in my times torn apart by mares eyes singed out
mercury in the wrong conjunction the moon a splot of blood
my father Lutheran himself go as mercenary in mud and snow
he killed Protestants in the Netherlands beat my mother
the sky crowded it seems with comets or deserted
a thousand disasters "against the stars"
ships at sea the wreckage in their wake
the whole world it seemed without mercy and burning

> and now I turn my eye to other lands the seas
> swarming over us swimming with bright fish
> kippers I could say but do not
> I am Kepler sick man I do not
> make jokes they think except they are
> the stars and I a skipper sailing through
> spirits direct and turn in the wake singing to us
> we are skippers in a bright bright sea
> though Tycho whirrs me round him like a slingshot

I have seen the turnings of stars
the perfect tunings God has inscribed there
the heavens humming with tops and I have seen
storms wash over coasts and whole cities
the storms that swoop peasants into revolutions
the planets wide murmurings have marked
how the Turks glimmer in blood at the horizon
murmurs in our hearts and I have studied the red planet
steadied it in its bloody socket

> one day, before, with my students

it is July 19, 1595,
                    and I am speaking

                        it is all I can do
            not to say finders keepers
                    but that would be silly
            my fingers where they point & pick

                        nets I say   nests
                conjunctions   Saturn and Jupiter
            pass through eight zodiacs from one
            trine to another trine and it is thus I
            inscribe circle within circle
            triangle with triangle look I say
            how it all falls into place
                    it is all there everything
                        so elegantly untangles
            and there is something like a tingle
            only giant and slow in enormity such elegance
            such beauty my children don't you see
            the birds the swift bright birds how they
                        wheel & cry

how the earth in its orbit measures all things
how within its dodecahedron Mars circles
and in Mars' tetrahedron a circle holds Jupiter
and Jupiter cubed contains a circle Saturn is

the sweep the beauty of it I had hoped to find
and I write Galileo to tell him so, later
all the long slow couplings and uncouplings

look now how it all fits together look I say
                    it locks
                            & unlocks

            here

                             & here

   & here

                                      & here

listen you can hear murmurs of the cosmos
murmurings in our hearts children
an icosahedron from earth puts Venus in a circle
Venus within an octahedron puts Mercury into another circle
that is the beauty of it do you not see my children
souls that steer the seven stars perfect as birds or fish
only the circles bulge to ellipses and there are rumours
there are wars and tumors loom into sight in the sky
                         what is this

                I, Kepler, feel so
      helpless
                 and so stricken

you have the reasons for the seven planets
              how one body fits so
exactly into place among the others how god moves
in perfect harmonics don't you see the morning
stars singing together the luminous signs

over the broken and bloodied body
singed wings the winds with cinders soldiers stir
         how Europe is a little girl
        bends to kiss Africa
        its severed head
the weeping house earth has become
             the shingles we crouch under loud with blood

letters

                in all that
        you had time to listen
        sounds of your thoughts going away

sometimes loose newspapers in winter
sometimes your hand over paper
your hair at night collar undone
night and day thoughts crawling to you

sometimes the way your body would
kick in you think by god it's a furnace
lungs rumbling away with air & it's good
the blood chugging the system
it all gets blurred   & rubbed

            & i write
                        letters
        dear father
                dear linda
        one letter after the other
            what are you doing
        dangling away on the afternoon
        listen dear daughter gangly as april
when will you wake   how is the baby i will
see you soon dear people where are you phil now
what do you look like elaine son uncle allen cousin
how are you aunt dear meggie my love my mother

            they never reach you
            they never do

        dear god where are you
        you wish you could now
it is   far off write listen listen where

                  & they could
          see you
there at the far borders parks are in
               wave
       ,palely
   take care you write take care

              write them
where are you are you   how if only
      i know   yes   letters
             what are you saying
your faces going
       i will see you soon
  & please write thinking of you
                   dear god
      how are you

home again

to come back to
          dogs barking
  sharp in morning
           coffee &
             someone
  calling for you
brick warm in the sun
         & bread

       your son's sweatshirt
       after hockey

       the sound of you
moving sweetly to day or to love
       your body on mine

       how when we were away
   the pull we fight we cling to
    grand mother lover we love
 & though it appears never leave her
     think we will wave to her
   circle in delight & adoration
      but how will she know
       we are waving
     where death in our hearts
       waits for us

earth when it gives
       mushy in march as oatmeal
       scrape of wind
       & the phone
rings you to come back
     to your senses
       come back
   to earth

how good to be
              returned to ourselves

        this our ever flowing
        ever flowering earth

        how fine how new
        the only home we have
        or will have ever

From *burglar of blood*

crewel work

embroidered our borders, our bodies
the deft needlepoint I bring
you in your parlour your pallor
you could be a lamp, shaded

no lady i feel no malevolence nor offer any
I always knew how you rose
how you would -rise ,silent as bread
deaf I thought at first you held
& inspected closely turned it
over & over were you astonished i could do
     would do it at all
     did you think how ill
     bred it is a tall
man with needles & thread at the door

were you so bored it would
excite you perhaps it does not
matter I saw it bring a scarlet
kerchief to your face yes though
hand to throat, cheek, you tried to cover
your eyes the quick light, then away
what is in them what do you hide

there is a swish of skirts & you saying
come in come in you say, me at the door
tall shadow at your feet the clock
tock tock dock duck talking in the woodflesh

you stand on your soft soft shoes
the tendons stand out the boundary
we feel all over our faces come in
you say please won't you come in
teeter on the faint fragrance your body gives
the way you let it off, fruit from a bowl

say something why don't you say something

　　　　your world　　　　I step into　is
not the crystal palace though it could be
lined with porcelain with a certain
uncertainty it could be a teapot i step inside

should I stop i should stop
sounds in your body quicken
the heat ticking the ticks between us
the air goes funny & tick tick tick
like that: an engine cooling
the anguish or injury you may do
　　　　　　oh do not put your fingers in
　　　　　　the engines of your dreams

only not, it's a stove more than anything

there is a smell in your clothes i smell
warm sun where you have been sitting
hear restless animals mew & brood
under the pillow in your boudoir

please you say please
　　　come in　why don't you
me a tall shadow tottering
　　　　　　uncertain caller
& then in, in, i fall in where we do not
　　　breathe the air is so thick i
　　　　　　yes you sway say yes undress
the garlic braid & then I very
　　　　　　gently very
　　　　　　　　slowly I
　the two braids, brown
　　　　　please i say you say
　　　　　　　please
　　　　　open the collar

          hang the two
          hot stings ,ear
     rings, place the red lace
          choker my elegant needle
     point you wear your neck under
               wide as a lake

     & then the six birds
on your neck take turns
     talking in your throat

From *goldfinger*

two thirds of the sun

> everything a haze heat a slur across
> my face everything
> a blaze, smell of spruce in heat

> leave the others at the foot the horses
> jangling, flies shiver, horses grazing.
> Michael and the others sing, sip beer, talk.
> The way he gazed at me as I told.

Pull my curiosity my future
up the rocks, up the mountain
climb until the moon is a wheel
smell of moon at 830

hand over hand I pulley my blood up
blood turns rubbery under the moon
goofy in lop-sided grin
body a hot water bottle I haul
at the end of a yo-yo moon
its wide-open yawn saw the moon
throw a rope round tomorrow
& hoisted it up the wall

Climb all evening, all night long,
for what I may find, and fear I will.

> The woman still reaching for the udder,
> the young man, wart on his left cheek,
> about to pull hairs out of the curry comb.
> The chicken stopped in mid-step,
> rust stuck in its throat,
> a pump seized up with its water song.
> There is even a pail fallen from the kitchen
> window there in mid-air it has stopped, amazed,
> 100 years ago the fire fallen

asleep the spider about to bite
the fly howling in silken finery,
only not, held there every
thing asleep everything inside its breath.
the start of recognition painted into the girl's face.

Even the wind, the wind swallows itself,
like a bottle. The whole place is a spider
on the bottom of a line forever drop us from dreams.

dropbydropbydropbydrop

*

have heard the stories how the wise women
came blessed the child and a thirteenth left
out because there was no room there
was no plate for her there were only twelve.
Left out left over she takes what is left to her,
they always do, resenting the young beauty.
A story into which the girl is taken
falls dead at fifteen, falls dead from a prick.
Yes, that is what the story says.

> I didn't write it.
> Nor did you.
> we have only to read
> as it was written.

> Only they don't tell that part
> now they say I am a figure
> who wears power in his belt
> sticks privilege into his hat.

I tell you how I hack my way
through thorns how thorns turn
into flowers part as I walk through
past bodies of young men impaled
torn open under the moon's bright eye
have thrown themselves on the barb
wire life is held in or out by.

They don't tell you about how they lie
dried fruit dried flowers
dozens of them juiced out sucked empty by sun
how their eyes are pecked out by crows
as they are dying dry into paper,
the privilege of death their bodies take on
on the way to a briar cemetery.

Nor do they tell how uncanny as dream
the palace lies without breath
not a bit of breath along the wet walls
so near death so close to me and far

—walk inside my body's sounds
whip of clothes against clothes
bodies dripping from time like banners
can hear my clothes snap when I walk by
could hear a moth walking in this cloud
this unknowing. Think of Michael, waiting.

*

                    I know what they say
             that I come, male, a smile poised
                inside my rights sweep the pale
                    girl onto her feet where when
                        she wakes she weeps.

You know the impediments of thorns,
smile, knowing I should enter through flowers.
Some of you say she is comatose,
preserved rose, perfect emblem of what I seek,
see my arrival only as violation,
pleasure taken, power proven.

*

                    This is what I find:

                    the whinnies spilled stones
fall out of horses scatter at my feet,
shivers where flies dart to surprise
as if they had never stopped the fire
gasps again against its breath the dogs leap
out into barks the chase the chickens
                    that walked their century
                    -old dream walked in the dream
                    for the dogs for the chickens
step down into scratch & cluck slightly dazed
the mill goes click clack click clack
as if it cannot believe it is turning
the ducks gather up their feathers
follow them into shade that drops
sudden from the walls behind
which they switched on the sun

                    into the yard the release of dream from dream
                    the way they all look at me look
                    at one another shake themselves
                    loose their bodies unlock pop
                    free they could be buttons coming
                    undone their eyes snap open are windows
                    as if they had just remembered
                             the world might unhinge
                             might move again before wind
                             slide open grinding against green

                             *

but before that this is what happens:
                             lean over to kiss the lips
                                cold as an estuary
                                yet I must do this this
                             is why I have come why
                                        i was sent

Perhaps the young men tried to break through
that the roast might sizzle, the flies might crawl
that men & women might meet in stables
that girls in scullery might eat fried drumsticks
that people might wade time
wake to time happening over & over again.

Know only the old man said
you must kiss her you must
kiss the briar girl he said
when you find her years from now
they will tell stories on you
and yet you must do this.

You will not want to do this the old man said
and he is right, I do not want to.
It doesn't help when I find the girl
frog-belly white from the years that drained her
tartared teeth, clothes soaked with water
stains all over her face, mineral deposits on a pump
and I could be back with Michael, drinking, talking.
stories of horses & music & women

*

Lean over the wax, answer to chemicals
the world swirls within, lethargic as a slug,
a thick mucous, to awaken
she does not want this either wants
only to sleep to lie still
clear as aether
to be winter no more
than wind when it is clear
there is no wind

Blow on the others too, though they are
not pleased either, altogether,
I blow their stillness off them
cause them to move, waken them into death.

*

Have only this excuse, that I have
left my friends down the hill that fields
when they turn over smell of earth
and in fall of wheat ripening

this is why I do it that milk
maids might milk that cows give milk
that at night when the moon is out cows jump
each month floods
reliable as a carburetor
oestrus erupts, bloody egg,
do it for the family of red
wing black birds that drop
into you every summer to feed

*

do it because it brings us around
two thirds of the sun
because when the moon closes
its eye I watch
the mascara of your sleeping

2

1995–1996

From *love in a dry land*

gotten so that's all I think
awake all night long
the window wide open
my eyes wide open

and I think of the ravine
a small crack in the prairie
the tall tall grass
hear their quick fever

the dark shrubs bunched up
under night thick
& squabbly as rhubarb
night smells stuck to the shrubs

know there are turtles heavy as field stones
moons so full with eons they would betray your neon blood
snails in their languor
the sloughs soupy with frogs
a sweet slipperiness in their cries

think how we would
slip down through
where day throws a beige
shawl over the banks
day's discretion

and where you go
into the blind night

ₚlop   ₚlop

PLOP

frogs smell of water
at the bottom, standing
it smells to high heaven

*

the moments you love
the Fuller brush

man oh man
he ups & enters
the contours of your days

in the fall the brush man comes & my
oh my your days are counted

dust shifts over everything table counter window
sill dresser silver mirror silk bed vanity
spread over everything light from somewhere
whizzes off his windows till you squint
and then there he is behind
the curtain his tin
lizzie black curtains and all
a drizzle of smells
tumbles out when he   opens
the door &
the light
speckles   /inside of a dog's mouth

oh oh you think one thing's
certain it's curtains for me

from out of travel zip
justlikethat he unzips
miracles reaches in and lays them
there on the table with the caramel sun
look at this bottle after bottle
bright hankies from a drawer or hat
the clinks and shades escape

you take and hold to the light
hold their collars in your hand
so many shapes and colours bright as blushings
so smooth in your hand so cool

                    Mr. Raleigh man Mr. Watkins please
                    call me Herb he says
                              or Buck will do &
                    there are brochures

                different names you feel
            excited to touch vanilla coconut spearmint
            pepper banana red bandanas you imagine
            he whips out & wears cinnamon lemon extract
            silk peppermint chocolate almonds cloves nutmeg
            come into the air into my burning ear he passes
            them the kitchen turns parrot green & sour
            everything concentrates you take purples & oranges
            stir their bright taste out in a glass
            Steven puckers his mouth and gulps

        oh mister vanilla villain listen I'm all ears
        all yours speak to me my maker of con
        fection fiction sweet talk the spices
        you bring riding across ocean across spacious deserts
        where's our camel mister what about the dates
        we could be living in caramel sin we could be
        up to our ears in carnelian a clear case
        of chalcedony don't you think
        i mean is this specious or what

rush me brush me off my feet why dont you speak to me
in the green laces somewhere across breezes from the
ocean air in my heart whizzing canaries & leaves bigger
than Mrs. N's suspicions so big no one can see under we
could take off faster than a pump car your shaving lotion
trailing noisily behind you hollering louder than caruso
I've half a notion let's shed sun why don't we shed
reticence like dirty clothes enter shade cool as shale &
citrous wet on our skin let's take off forget those drippy
caraganas let's go where carloads of carob trees &
big-lobed carnauba trees wheeze chlorophyll in your
face & air is thick as rum & yr hair in the late afternoon
shines like cellophane how chic i think we could carouse feel
all the 8 bones in the carpus believe me that's what you do

                                                    87

in the caribbean

                              salves liver pills kidney pills
                         powders toothpaste camphor soda
needles buttons that are oval & black & burn holes in your
hand square ones that feel thick & will never get lost
made of wood & brass & bone coarse thread silk
  thread cotton string in yellow & red & blue plaid paisley
you see herringbone neat as fish without the flesh things
in thimbles mouse traps and red waists on corn brooms
    scissors that feel nice in your hand bright files & knives
inlaid with letters and long handles for cutting everything
& ladles in six shapes stiff mops & floppy mops &
                    ammonia zippers that make quick

  sounds yes sounds crazy but yes you can any length
you want or colour their swift little gasps and giggles
everything the ladies want you say look at this paste waxes
    liniments of desire he said in the book pink powder
furniture polish that lingers in air shampoo in burnished
columns brushes & you can smell the new wooden
handles smooth things for teeth & nails & cattle & floors
  the living room grows fuller & fuller your cheeks grow
warmer in tonics perfume with names like Spring Lane
Lavender & Green Sea Spray & Glen Mist soap in its own
boxes & fits your hand hair cream in tubes you can
squeeze or bottles you shake out the lustre & clinks
              bubble bath that comes in big seeds

                    all these wonders the trays open out
                  all this drives up to the door and spills
                all this in a little suitcase full of travelling

& there is one bottle solid & discreet as
the deacon you think may well come undone
brown in a daring yellow cap & apron

              HERBS
                  it says

and when it speaks
fills your palm with
shiny brown buttons

*

r r r r r r r r - r r r r r r r r r - r r r r r r r r r r - r r r
someone cranking
voices inside the phone
kerosene lamp its gentle talk
a yellow shore i sit
knit knit knit
pull the yarn into small bridges
someone giving up on grief

HELLO i say hELLO
HELLO you say HELLO
i say IS IT YOU
3 long, 1 short
ARE YOU THERE

something acid on the air
acrid in my ear
katie angus listens in anger
hoping to wring scandal out of the phone
watches the receiver as if it were a sundial to heaven

all night long the ragweed is shrinking
flowers closing their throats
thirsty for morning the yellow oil
weeping into the yard the goose tapping
her loneliness at the pane

imagine you out there
the long windy night
the long purple nerves
wiring us together

*

horses out there
grazing on darkness
night a pasture
they dream in, standing

& when they dream
do they dream of running
past the wind running
through an electric sun
night jingling from their halters

do they gauge
sugar in wind
gazing at the blue frogs
their dark eyes gouged out

El Greco lying still
& stiff as forever
strange grin on his face
ants cleaning in his teeth for eternity

nights I lie naked
grass the sky full
eyes staring down
open as stars, as uncaring
the moon tied
shut with wet needles & thread

& days I fold
a sadness into
as i do your clothes
when I hold them

& the wire on the fence
sags from the weight of sun

*

the morning after
it is clear and bright
so bright you could see
forever it seems
only your eyes hurt
the whole world is coated
the whitest white
Jan 31 & 30 below
a wedding cake
someone's smeared

snow squeaks when you walk
it protests it does not
like to be stepped on
then the joy the foot
warmer under the robes
the world polished with cold
you can see forever

later that day
we are on our way
back from the Benson parish
Philip and I ride up over
the world around us turning blue
stark & blue as electricity
night close that close
everything seems
to have shut & perished

the Harneys' rise horses snuffing
harness jingling so clear
it could be the beginning of the world
the runners break the crust
the day bleak and cold now I
could weep almost for loneliness

I was thinking we could stop
at the Lennochs' for a cup of tea
yes Philip I would like that
that would be nice

and then over the crest
the sudden sprawl
off to the right
the red & white
the double shock
a wagon, old cart,
high narrow sides
in the ditch /tipped
a dozen legs in the air
lying there like spilled toys
all those cattle frozen solid
where they drifted on storm

*

this is in fall

flowers, their sore throats

paul so dusty
            with talk
        i should
rinse him out with tea

            this is in fall
            this is when grass
                    ripens to smoke

*

by the gosh i just waltzed him
right clean through the prairie
just as smart as you please
no if's and's or maybe's
right straight through the eyes
hopping all round us
faster than frogs in rain
snappy as buttons popping off

boy oh boy we were going
to set the bottom of the world on fire
the prairie too if i had
anything to say about it

is that right i say
is that right

From *Irene*

thought you would live

so long   i would die

before you,
hardly   thought
this , then

thought of   you
holding me   still
at   my death

still as threads in a shirt
no one is wearing

still as a table
no one is at

the time you put me
into music & lights

we would turn inside them
we would turn counter-clockwise
i remember
every time you rolled into sight
on my right
my mom & dad
i wanted to whirl
out of the music & lights
turn off all the sounds & colours
turn them all inside out

so there would be you & me
& my dad
the light & the music inside
the bright music & lights

wanted to
be thrown against you
the way grasshoppers went splot on windows
when you went fast & you smelled wheat
smelled hot grasshoppers on the grill

farm boy on a wooden horse
goes round & round
goes up & down
all the small children
careen on a carousel
solemn & scared

the time you put me
into time & took me out

thanks giving

in the fall
night slams shut
frost bangs & bangs all night long wants in
night could be an abandoned building
its doors swinging loose in wind

next day the yard is wet
a gentle slant the sun takes
you always loved & were touched by
even in the ferocity of estevan sun
its velocity you moved a life through
you spent your garden swimming in it
talking to yourself & the carrots
the tomatoes you took in every fall
orphans from summer

next day we tread the light the nights ruin
look it is easy i can keep afloat mother
though the yard is empty of summer
you every summer threaded there
and the house is empty of you

you are not here you are
under the frost they pull over
you on a hospital bed
St. Joseph's where you bore each of us
where Dana & Megan were born
your feet purple with varicose veins
they could be egg plants
they could be flowers

step out Sunday morning among
plants night has squashed
some bloated some limp
a few of them slump like tired babies

the zucchini are still there
buttoned to their rinds like underwear

tomatoes sag into their old skins
sing with blood in their throats
the dirt dries under foot harder
than ever heat could make it

it is thanksgiving we are home
you are not here you are sick
& still you bestow
carrots potatoes tomatoes
the back yard falling
like a bombed-out building
into death we are filling
up with cold when we are home
we will eat what you have given
feast on what you planted
the sharp juice in our mouths

soon the garden will shine with frost
hard with cold, white as cancer

-

you have carried your death

      with you all your life
    carried it carefully as a flower for years
    you cared for us let us sit in under
the garden of your tending

& then the explosion that hits
your body a sun
throwing off bits of life
like sun spots, pollen

              a wild growth,
                dying

            now when you
              let it

                   go

        it will not
          let you   go

      in hollow walls & hallways
          it will hold
      you a wide-eyed angel
         terrible in its hands
          the white angel will take you
               with it
          it will never
        leave you
          it will not let you
        alone

        not though you wrestle
        not if you bless it
    or curse it

: the garden of your body we feed on

-

mother tongue
       we learn
           to speak
    yearn to talk

at our mothers breast
we learn to say things
you coax us into

      take our first
shakey
         steps
into speech

play air
     again
  & again
     try to speak
       our mother
    tongue tied
        so to speak

inside this room
    tied to you
we try &
     nurse you
back to breath

can hardly
     talk
hardly say
  a thing
dare not
  breathe
a word

-

there is a small boy he is five maybe four he is dressed in
darkness he is wearing brown rayon pants & shirt to
match his mother has just bought

he is squinting into the sun light falls off his face onto
paper he leans over 40 years later rubbing darkness
from his eyes but now he is mad he does not like these
clothes does not want to be in the picture his eyes hurt

it is the end of a hot day the sky is open behind him in
front too except for the pumphouse frighteningly
small at his back in the picture he is facing into the sun
into the camera the long shadows tethered for 40 years
you are holding fall out of your hands as only in the
prairie they could your own long shade stands in you
on the other end you want to take him into the camera

he likes the shadows how steep & strong the time you are
sliding down though he does not know this either nor
why you want the picture nor that you are feeling time
pressing with the sun at your back he does not care
you want this perhaps his hair is newly cut it might
have been this may be why he does not want this he
hates the bits of hair on his neck

he knows there is a garden to your left outside the picture
behind the picture the corn in forests above him there
would have been a garden there would have been all
you hoped the day you take the pictures and behind
you the days you dreamt this day that would ever enter

behind you at the end of the lane he will hear a voice a
few years later a clear voice out of the sky strong and
clear this will be the end of day one summer the large
sun hung in the west bright bird in its nest every day
forever a door closing in shadow he will hear what it
says he will ask did you hear it too though when he is
a lot older he will not remember what it said the voice
though you will say no you did not hear when he asks
you then

he will remember where you stood in front of the sun the
small spot where your body will begin to boil over you
want to coax a mother's picture from him he will
remember there were long shadows distinct as faces
long as memory as slanted

there is sun in his eyes
where you stand in front of the sun
you have disappeared into over
-exposed to time & the picture
they never took of you

you went into the picture
before they fell out of your hands
& you were dissolving
turning to light, losing your shadow

−

all the letters   you sent
they fell   into silence
month   after month
snowflakes   into our yard
your love   loneliness too
the way we   fell out
from under   you
at times you sent   that too

disguised it all   in talk
wrote   gardens   neighbours
family   weather   politics

and though we phoned   drove home
never wrote back   almost never
a few times   the last few years
& never once did I

tell you what   I meant to, quite
though I   know you knew

though as you wrote   you did not
know for years cancer is a snow storm
that it blows inside you and you are caught
in it you will perish of cold
die from white out
nor do you know
I will write these letters
when you cannot read them

-

Estevan cemetery
                July 13,
arc of one year   july to july
when you knew   when we bury you

the ravines below the hill
                hold water, greenness a generosity in them
                        they have not been this way
                        since we were small

                a sandy soil
                                —family graves
            all the rooms they forever lie in
                    the deep-lying dead
                under blue
                    grampa wilson
                where he took me
            i was, what, six
                    said this spot is for me
                here is one for your mother
                        how frightened i felt
                                    & sick
                the birds flying over, in wind

                    : a wild grass
                purple flowers sideways
            half feathers on the stem
        patches of it, cemetery spotted with it
                                , its delicacy
                small modest blossoms
        "blue gamma" Lorne says when Diane holds it up
        "gramma too"
                        /"blue gramma"

                    Dana moves off
                this is not her gramma
                the one she knows is nowhere

in what the minister
new from down East, young
seeks to say what cannot be said
says what millions have said
will say

my uncle Oris turned 85 into a place
memory has left
time has led him into a bewildered face
Ann what are we doing here he says
what are we doing here Ann

From *passwords*

a hole in your blood

for 36 years i knew you
married your blood
         carried it
quietly around you

the way a father might
carry a sleepy child
a glass at night
         thin bottle
shines, a kind of halo
         36 years
fell in waterfalls your blood

silent as silent movies
     when music isn't
or snow when you are inside

one of those globes we had
some landscape in it, ferns & coral

the way when you tipped snow would fall
so thickly so gently you did it again & again

& in it all the wreckage
            your seasons
kept coming & coming

& sometimes before you fell
more & more silent embraced us
   in food & silence

        more & more
your blood fell ringing around us
like suspenders, loosened, an umbrella

              / snapt open
          a shade, shadow
    we could come in under

    at Niagara you never saw the boats go under
    your face fresh with spray & your arms

    you brought all the structures of your love
              carried them right up to the door

                  we picked them up
                    & you one day
                   blew a hole
                   in your blood &
           all the snowing
              stopt

he tries to learn the language

kuli Anna tells me *kuli herr cooley*
Anna who usually bewilders
me with her excited mimes
eager attempts to teach
german coaxings as if
she were pulling a string
out of me though i bob be
wildered as a bear must
knowing he is near
but cannot reach the honey

        Waschbär i know :
        "raccoon" yes & i live
        i really do on Ahornweg
        on "Maple Street" true
        north strong & free but

          was ist das Anna
    point to the table where i am
    writing daß ist ein kuli she says

    so the pen is a cooley & so
    is a chinese labourer
    Helmuth tells me at dinner

                cooley: a pen
                name a writer

       : a labourer
      , in german

he reads the map
(for Gene)

        frightening the way you snap
        open you could be
         a window
        after a long winter
               you open
        the map &

theres germany barbered & bare
   -bummed before you
      know what's hit
terrible with varicose veins
all of germany is one
big blood sausage

its aged & ravaged grammar
your parents' parents' bodies knew
& all over its body these huge splotches
bruises maybe or blood
clots that's cities who can tell
are you reading the map correctly

     you are all over
the map there are many signs
to many people how are you
to know who or where
           you are

                whiz past
           yourself in english
        map spread before you
         a starched table cloth
         everything 's spilt on
          it could be a mystery
           you are reading

why when you are so close
to your dear old gramma
doesn't someone say you are
here here you are but

you lose your place can't find
it can't tell is germany near
a coronary or is it
bleeding to death

Trip home, trying to read signs

                              squirk squirk
                  rain
squirksquirk

trans-atlantic

I suppose that's ok
what John said about him &
his girl they're set
in this strange compass
& when he's kicking around
she's this leg or a rim

& out he goes out she goes
whizz whizz *whir whir*
pulleys or wheels, fast things
arm in arm, leg in leg

somewhere over the North
Sea there's this joint see
where they come together

that's ok John he's got somethin' there
far as im concerned fine that's just fine
but with you & me lady i aint
got a leg to stand on & so
id say between you & me
she's well somethin' like

                              ,a yo-yo , say
you throw me off in a fast spinney sound

                    & then I up &   /
              reel back
                              real fast
    a cross the Atlantic
cross the sun blinking & sweating
way up the sky rowing its way to canada

wave as i whip past singing like a top
faster than Lindbergh faster
& faster hold your breath hold your
breath come whirling back again

home again to your beckoning
finger figure i hope to linger
the palm of yr hand sweet
sleep the steep slope
our night takes swimming
the dark way you clutch me
                    squeeze me
tighter than compression rings

strasbourg

a woman in gingham on a brass box is a fortune teller
wrenched through yr childhood the plaster lady even her
face is plaster as if it pleased her to be so chalky you swear
her eyes fixed on your eyes fixed on her the purple lady in
the glass booth her chipped hands dropping yr story the
pivots in wheels arms hands feet on and on this small box
we are enraptured she steps down to walk she is coming
unwound you can see the machinery her body trembles
over gears & meshes doesn't look at anyone oh girl of
mime her eyes are plaster they have lost their lustre she
cannot see she is not looking her eyes are blank colours &
sounds swing round & round the ferris wheel rolling onto
a bright blue estevan sky into the machinery of time she
steps into early july before them does not lose her, up,
balance jerks back back up onto onto into herself yanks
herself onto the box she has never left back the pivot she is
captured in halts starts sticks loosens she stops she is
trying to come undone where her step started down jerk
jerk she winches back up into rewinds on sun into a steep
sun beside the cathedral winds herself back up the lady
plaster lady on gears the smell of new hay you tossed
nickles to click click dropping the card you are to take in
your hand jerks halts jerks

& then it is over light dissolves in her still she was across
time running she flows back into now she is open as
evening & there is a small wind when she bows light
blows in we applaud reach coins into an open sky small
bits of it is June the sun is shining her eyes are grateful we
drop pieces of sun her springs were rusted in & came out
of water she is ordinary she is a miracle come back into
her eyes see she steps down stoops from her box for her
box look at how she is moving it is over it all drops off she
has returned brass hat in hand she has come back come
down from boxes that turned eyes saw nothing a lady in

glass in purple & white plaster robes on the hill under
the tree dropped cards into your hands at the Estevan fair
her hands told your story she was your guide you were
in her hands

the service out & now they come out of stone they step
into sun, slow, their eyes hurt, sun like wind in their eyes,
they could be stepping out of the Orpheum into an
Estevan summer, blinking, stemmed by the edge of light
and the man is the magician in front of the blue flag it is
his turn to disappear inside his machine to go inside
another man & another it is their turn to put faces on
paper there on the other side of the square the faces sit
happy they spread petals of light the artists put their
paper faces on the opening page & it opens spreads
colours out/

berlin

        step out at Savignplatz
walls covered with art
the artists area Kurfürstendam

south of us the display
the goods east germans walked past
will they learn to be godly once

they walk through a hole in the wall
gazers from a black hole
one day dazed, packed side by side
size by size in
                        utter silence
                         just looking
           mesmerized as the man
         nequins whose sequined pose they pass
         they stare in women behind glass stare back
         their wild red hair holds their eyes

         they are leaking into a silent movie
         extras on the set others star in
         all this streaming out of their heads
         something lacking in their eyes
         do they see any where
                      any thing at all
                       any sign
                themselves
                  in the windows
               looking back
             have they lost their voices
                    for good

gijon

walking fish market glass blown full with fish octopus
  huge squid delicate speckles and pink sheen crabs the
  smaller dark brown to charcoal and furry we ate
  yesterday big flat grey fish flat pink ones and the jagged
  spines all around and eyes on top man chops off with a
  cleaver and chops in half small transparent teeth shiny as
  wet plastic a long fish with faint grey skins smaller ones
  shaped like tulibees only flatter and redder a priest in
  full robes floats by shadow under the window cool
  behind the glass in front of you and dry ones curled on
  themselves like potato peels baskets of snails black shells
  large silver and charcoal sardines rainbow trout i think
  the man with huge scissors cuts open quick twist flick
  and the guts are gone prawns huge fish with saggy skin
  monkfish looking solemn some long fish skinned and the
  coarse flesh shows small flat white fish bright as light
  bulbs they could slip in your hands easy as oil and tuna
  after tuna the man heaves their hugeness up the
  enormous cleaver slices off gills head fins sluices the guts
  and blood slices the packed flesh snicks spine after spine
  each slice with the heel of the cleaver 3 sometimes 4
  people moving in an island of fish and the man throws
  ice back over glacial mounds holding it yes the faces nod
  yes yes cutting washing flash of their movement wrapping
  muscle writing flat slippery white ones flatter than slippers
  a slab is it halibut one large crab breathing upside down
  bubbles and clams hairy with sea weed are waving

on the other side banks of women have washed up on
  shore and they wave and reach their mouths open they
  are blowing something into air the men seem to be
  catching and taking in they are jostling for air spaces
  they look short and out of breath their arms signal
  dozens of arms waver in pinks and speckles soft-skinned
  and dazed to the men the island of fish they must sing
  silent songs calling them onto the shells and bones into

beautiful wreckage all the fish and men and women you
in the street in the window in the sun the sweet ocean
breeze the light the knives the men in white

driving

we passed the cows
every day shining
80 eyes that showed
their stomachs
where to go

brown rocks
shining
in grass

3

New Poems

let your rod be light

and very gentle
the best is of two pieces
and let not your line exceed

proper length I say
not more than three
or four hairs at the outside even

if you can play a little better above
in the upper part but if you can
manage to angle with one hair

you will have many more
rises and catch the eye of
many more above

all you must take care
not to take on too much and to hand
i cap yourself with too long a line

as many in mistaken pride do and be
fore you begin posit
ion yourself so

that the wind is at your back
and if there is sun to have it before
you always to work down

stream the tip of your rod down
ward modestly such
that the shadow from

you and your rod
will be least offensive for the sight
may well amaze them and spoil
your sport of which you must

take great care
and if you hit to make your fly
right and have the luck to hit also

where there is great store
a dark night a right wind
this from the south you will

surely grow more and more
in love with the art of fly
making more and more in love

with the natural fly
it is excellent and affords
much pleasure

---

whiskered Izaak in my ear
mouth full of fur and feather
on the fourth day

at night, staying with your grampa

the creaks in the camp cot we crawled
our sleepiness into my grampa
wilson & i kitty-corner from Valleyview
school where they held the sports days
& the yard was hard with cinders & sun
oranges at lunch you peeled your stomach
fluttery as a mother killdeer &
somewhere from upstairs they played
Under the Double Eagle on a scratchy record you
felt funny inside you skinned your elbow
but this is all

years later your grampa wilson is dead
& you don't sleep
by the splotchy shadows from his window
& when he is
in hospital dying of a strangulated hernia
the doctor won't come & so he dies & your mom
she stays at his place & cooks for everybody she makes
wonderful buns from Robin Hood flour butter
melts on & you
are shocked when at supper on the farm she starts
crying what will happen to mother she says

only this is when you are 6
there isn't yet a place he went into
there are not yet moments outside
your grampa is not dead is not
dying & you are not yet 7 you are staying
with your grampa every morning the russian
thistle you have learned he holds at the end the knob
shtropp **schtrrop**
stropp the long leather tongue he brings
brightness into   a shiney stick
psskps shshps it says the bar of silver
the blackness in his hand he takes you

fishing you like the way the big black
car goes over gravel into the dusty sunshine it slides
past sharpens against the car down into the valley
the way you find the corner at Possum's
you say grampa you should get a new car

you are playing possum you should not be here
(you have left your gramma behind in her smells
)only you realize years later they must know they must
let you & your grampa fish he is over 70
you are under 7 they let you fish & the fish
he yanks from his hand dangles
long as his forearm long as the day the long green

        that mysterious & beautiful muscle
        it lives under where kids drown
        the dirty souris & the flies
          on the river skin
              they skim from

        the trunk is coated with graveldust
                the fenders still
hot from summer in them & the smell
        the garage when day begins
thickens and goes limp the late after noon
            lines it with dust & cork
floats the fish from the trunk when you get back gramma
wilson in the other room in bed in lilac smells
           ever since you were

        one fish the musky smell starts
swimming when he is cleaning slips through
        hands the slime & then
at night there is crumbly cement
the basement wall comes off
        its dark coal smells
             & there is a case of coke

)it is starved for light too
        you brush it off
your face & you lie on the cot eyes wide

          there are moments   outside something
            moving you can   hear the curtains
                drop   slow shadows & they
            move shadows   on the far wall
            the alarm clock   shudders & talks
              tock tock tock   talks to itself

        all night long wide awake
the all night shadows are awake
                      your face you can hardly breathe
                      you wish you were home
                              you have fallen in
                      a dugout its slippery sides
                      you can't climb out
                      inside your new flesh you are
                      frightened you are 6 years

the clock   talks in the wood
it has dry   bones the clock
bones   and wooden sticks
you strike   together at school
embarrassed & they   call it music

                  your grampa sleeps beside you
                    his enormous cock how it
                          astonishes you
                          in the morning
                          when he pisses

courting

                        sure it may be
                            small & rubbery

                                it may be even
                                    resilient under pressure

                        thats no reason you have
                            to rub & treat it so

roughly slap it around
   redfaced & blubbery in front of the shrubbery
        & lash it in such grubby fashion
      back & forth back & so forth
      such a terrible racket he can see
thwack thwack you have a sweet spot
   for him his heart a squash or tennis
ball cross court on your whapwhap high
            strung laminated nerves

   you are courting disaster lady you are flying off
the handle (or on it)
                            day & night
   play the strings to his heart
      squelshed it & squeezed him in a most
   unladylike way till veritably he gasped
the grip you put on him & oh my lady him in
the way you heel & toe up shaft to throat

      you are so high and mighty
                    he has actually been ill
served he has been shafted by your daring
   returns & mind when its set to go off you
                            string him
      along he says darling
                    you play a base
   line game oh dear

               such comings & goings during
        the pigeon stutter of your majestic toes
               one-luv two-luv he says luv i for one luv
        when you lob or better still slam him to the back
               frankly he can hardly take your back
        handed compliments mind intent on the net
                      gain & back again
        the wriggle of your cute little tutu bum

but what he likes most of all
                      in the battering he takes
        in her genteel lime rickey ball game
                      is when
        she searches shrubs feverish for him
. for she is losing her grip .
                      he can see through
               her white
                      and well-bred clothes
        small zones of sweat
                           & heat

fenestration

down those roads in a red toyota
mile after mile shamble by in graveldust
ramshackle bones time has clicked
clean as lime flesh once lived on
rooms bloomed with kids & stinkweed & cows
livid as welts where barb wire ripped

the warm viscera of their coughs & kitchens
lungs soft and moist as night at night
the big dipper north star orion
sky a garden sown with stars
& onions in every darkness stands
inside a deep silence

their lantern hiss in night waters yards
pull from the earth dogs & separators
piled in pastures & dreams
that fall out of parlors
all this in rusted pails & pistons

gates time has opened & blown in
grit it leaves when it rubs talk out
buildings arthritis has happened in
lean over bend boney ears to hear

the yards have vomited themselves empty as wind
silent as paper planes a kid held once

before they fly
& after

the gunshot report of trees going off
40° below our hearts

home steading

there would be children
      bing bing bing
sixteen seventeen eighteen of em
just like pop corn
    she stirred round & round &
bang theyd go on the lid
& you know what that lead to

       there theyd be
this big bowl of them
   buttery things & sturdy as stools
      / & a mom

sometimes when sleep would peel
day off her face
          she must have dreamt
  it was a cold cream night

they squished their blood past
rubber boots theyd overflow the kids
when they cross the night & its spring
water so cold it stuns or it scrapes
what little heat there is off
them & the stove

her eyes would look
& study those children
she would be homesteading
before long she would be home
where children streamed
      by & screamed

     the wind &
      the sky flapped
   wildly held her hands
  fresh laundry she hung

on rungs of sun on the bed to dry
where the earth sweats beside her

megan

,waiting

our lives thin & precarious as light
when bulbs puncture they end
time rattles inside & wears through
explode when dropped or run
over or wear down after awhile
filaments flimsy as nerves

you on the end of our lives
something is in & they will enter
the thin membrane of your breath
your life that lifts from our throats
wanting you to float there forever
moving as moons should move
      bright & perennial as the night which turns
                  into a second fullness
      stuck on the sky's high ceiling
                  our silent calling

                  blue moon the man on radio says
            this is once
                  in a blue moon

      the warm & uneven way we stand
      the uncertain waiting our breath takes
      seeing you thrown onto the world's four winds
                  far & fast as weather
                  the seasons blowing through

      no way to pull you out or hold you
      here at the end of the string
      luminous as the sky in our hands

windy weather in all of us
not knowing which way the winds are blowing
    or when they will end

        *

    night before:

three when you wakened screaming
the wolves are eating my stomach
only you couldn't say the "l" quite
said wo'ves are eating my stomach
you in my arms knowing they held you
against everything forever

lie now inside your fear
something again is eating your stomach
& you wonder though do not say is it
what ate your grandmother away
fear has thrown its switches &
a small bomb has gone off inside
& Fenrir i know is eating the moon
is eating you yellow as the jaundice
you were born into Christmas

tomorrow they will go inside
our fear the cold in the room your small body
my father's hands i touch you with
what i know you feel at our skin
would lift this from you now
let you into sleep where you hear
my body running over

we both know there is nothing i can do
cannot scare off the wolves this night
which always before you have turned

to anger now you lie quiet
at the ends of my frightened love
      allow my hands
move into sleep under my face

                    *

dream of you as freckles:

    shallow plate of your breath
shadow sparrows drink at, startled

                              i am thin as tin
                             the smallest word
                                could puncture
                             everything dust so
                               dry i could fall
                            almost with the pain
                              & still feel i am
                                so transparent
                                you could see
                                right through
                                    see wind
                                 on the other
                                        side

              *

        night :

                             the sleep you have
                            bandaged yourself in
                               fish in the dark
                                     waters

coming back into
your flesh
rising in
day

*

were you cold

you looked cold
you say

last night

*

, morning of

your mother climbs the dawn
the bright wires in the streets
the last days of august swing open
more large & open than ever this summer
in the morning to braid your hair
against all unravelling to tie up ends

in whose body month after month moons drifted
till one caught
& there was you

sounds of morning rise
our shadows on the wall
sun across your bed
you hold yourself in
your body
blooms brightly
with fear

though this is the seventh hour of the seventh floor
there is no one to climb your long hair to rescue
nothing to keep out the snow
not the wooden christmas decoration
our want of you hangs by the mirror in
no not your robe blue as may nor your nose
where you thought you were broken
not even your hair to protect you

                    the emptiness
                              of your sandals
                  when you go

                        *

      megan, in

            , the morning we go down into
everything fragile , the air
            its yellow feel
        always i loved this time of year
                    the gentle
                clarity of light
            brittle this time
ice the water's drained under

                    in the streets people move
            oblivious to time almost
everything so slow
                              so fast
a dream you cannot want

you are alone in a room full of strangers
who touch your loveliness with a strange love
                    a man's skilled & clumsy hands
            write scars over your unknowing
            puts holes in you wanting you whole

in this world they take things away
when the winds blow moons through our hearts
our hands feel the weight of your skin not there

                    *

came to braid the morning
    as they did the queen's
                        , her hair
    preparing for death

                    *

            you lie there

            eyes beneath

        all that darkness

its weight on your eyes

love western style

sure sure I got it looket that
the envelope 's right here
[smacks his left shirt pocket
a little explosion of dust, or smoke]
a cowboy sort of expression laconic
as whiskers or a mickey of whiskey

see that got er tucked away real nice
neat as Aunt Elvina's false teeth
got this here red velvet
case made special in Montreal
& she 's stayin put   ee-YUP
[pause to roll a cigarette, one hand]

yyyup takin er thru pony exPRESS
can hardly find a way to express
all the way this pink & perfumed
thing you have sent me with
coz I am everywhere

faced with such attacks & envy
such force of wind & sand
my skin lopes clear
across the burning [lights
a match on his jeans]

plains we elope loop we rope
[match to cigarette smoke
from nostrils] in all the wind
& sun scalding as fried tomatoes
us ripped on sun we sip
our loopy & rowdy lips madam
burning you on my lap fragrant
[closeup cigarette stub

my mom wants me to come in for the night

the yellow stuff inside the windows fluf fluff it goes
fFlufF fluffluff jennie jennie they say you have to pee the
kids up and down the sky when it gets tired and gets dark
up and down up and down came the doctor in came the
nurse and splot splot spills all dirty goes dark in came the
lady in yellow pudding the big fat purse smooth smooth
but not bad old stinkmilk the table mom puts big green
things the crinkle things and white stuff you bite the
round things brendan says here the new baby when mom
takes his clothes off stinky mom says hes soiled only you
bite the squeaky parts inside you bite and echh your
mouth it is funny when it happens and then jimmy he
pinches nyya nyaa nyaa nya nNYA im tellin jimmy im
tellin mom girls are such sucks youre gonna get it splot
splot spit him youre stupid youre stupid jimmy hansen
jiim-ee jim-EE stuuu-PID jimmy dirt on his foot things for
heaven sake you two jimmy the dirt pushes will you stop
it you two and white stuff she sticks where my hand leaks
and there is a squeak he takes from his a place under there
hey look jennie makes clicky sounds looket what i got
suns in them click click you see right into them the nuns
said thats where god is jennie a litle drop of oil my dad
spills round round and he watches only jimmy no jennie
le'em alone he spoils it fly away fly away fly away and
after there is brown sugar and cinnamon and slippery
from a door my mom finds and its open face falls off don't
touch hot hot on me and there is sticky little sticks you
slap sticks and stones may break my bones jimmy sounds
uncle brendan says when they put a shiney stick in his
mouth and the floor is shine yellowy they stick to you my
mom says poor brendan he has a bad heart and they give
you the man with the thing from his throat my mom looks
funny her face goes fluffy im ascared and it says its ok
jennie its ok

silver nitrate

thats you third from the left the light thuds in you the
thots you blink though you are not there yet you are
talking your mother is one row behind and two to the left
she is dressed in light blue you can see though it is black
and white and she smiles through as she listens to you
almost she remembers you spoke to her on the streetcar
she is 12 and there is a crescent under each finger nail
quick dirt you took on easy as sun and as rash pilled the
threads to her thoughts piled them up till you are saying
something on the seat beside and she closes her eyes

your face is wobbly this day all alone you get on it is
always wobbly and today it says no no it will be all right
billy but i don wanno go i don wanna die bunches of
water and shiney bits the clank-clank machine squeals like
pigs when you let blood out and puts you your face says
you will be ok billy dont worry they will look at your
tooth and then you will come home ok i don wanna die
mom they let the blood out the men cloud up all the ducks
and bugs and green stuff and cold gets in and it is stiff all
over

she does not say cannot say you were sick when you were
born almost died carried the curves in what happened
past her care beyond any curing and that later that day
after the photo the faces turned toward the light trustful
as flowers they wait in the sun some wilt some tilt and
then your father comes out & goes under the hood leaves
it kneels beneath the dark felt he takes you into so
whaddya say billy go for a paddle and get us some fish eh
a rub where his hand is your hair you like ok ok dad

> on your own you bike wave shake
> your fist at cars their fastness

and there you are now in my sticky hands thats you
third from the left the picture now you wink from blood
that drifts across your face
the deltas your wrists are were
cracks of light you crawled into
& out of

                         and after the marshes your light went out in
                            a slash in time you sank like a shot frog
                               intense as marsh gas billy and as slight

                               we dredge your sleep
                    and your mother behind the smile
                    years later behind your face or time
                              weeps for what never happened

twice a year

twice a year i wear my father's skin
each may every october i climb
into his skin shrug & turn
the seasons over, nothing to it
clockwise, that's spring
counter-clockwise &
it's fall
a few twists of the pliers,
a new season
the plumbing in   ,or out

a kind of bear i guess except
my father wore these clothes
closer than words
when he started up
the machinery of seeds in spring
when he let may into the farm
& every fall let summer out
drained it, heat in the radiator
a leak in the year he opened
the green tractor
when you got home late
& it was dark in the yard
eyes ript out of summer
& he yanked a plug in the dark
& the cold cursing

a bit like letting a cat out for the night
into claws & whiskers whatever
suspicions of mice slept in its throat

once a year i plug the cottage in
five months listen
to a summer birds simmer in

late afternoon begins
& drags the birds out, their brightness
    & then once more
unplug it, hopeful as a farmer
at harvest & seeding lets water into place

    but trees
get tired & the heat drips out
        leaves dry as paper

sadder in fall maybe than he was
though who can tell what winter
held for him how winter held him
    bright at the window
        when he climbed out
       coveralls stiff at freeze-up
      & when he climbed back in

this was when melting happened when
he climbed back into spring & wondered
where the water went when he turned around
& it was 20 below morning

every year my dad drew lines

he may as well have drawn lots
but he never did he always drew lines
           lots & lots of them

into the land these long long lines
he would go bumping down the lane
first on the Massey & then the John Deere Dear
John he would write inbetween
           scribbled in that
stubby scrawl of huge fingers
      thick from nicotine & grease & tools
he wrote his hand over the face of the earth

              every spring he went at it writing spring
              dear spring darned glad you came back
              all winter I was wondering where you'd gone
              wrote flax wrote wheat hello
              wheat hello wrote dear barley
              seeds brought out the author in him

              wrote rapeseed once but it didn't
              write back a lot of his correspondents
              never replied some years
                    he hardly heard a thing
              he'd drag those pencils across the fields
                & wait & wait
                          & wait
              he wanted to keep in touch

      in good years when he left his homework on the black
            boards wrote between the lines
                sun rhymed
                  seeds green with june then
                          blond as august

this was when they carried on
some kind of correspondence
before he wrote them off altogether

    most years the seeds fell silent
    sometimes they'd mumble a bit
    sometimes they'd hardly let out a peep
    when they stopped talking altogether
    we moved into town it gets lonely
    talking to yourself

                god knows
    he yearned for a word from them
    any word wondered had his letters
    never got through was it the wrong
    address had the earth moved left
    no forwarding address every spring
    my dad wrote them in a fever
    he was in love these were love
    letters he wrote every spring had they
left him for another couldn't they give him a call
my father grew more & more hurt they didn't answer

every spring my mother poked spring

her finger was a pencil
she wet & rubbed seeds off

in no time they were singing back potatoes
lettuce tomato carrots cucumber shouting
the whole yard a squabble of vegetables
a fox among hens could have done no better
you couldn't sleep nights for their sighs & yelps

the frogs began to move
out they couldn't
hear themselves think
would have died off
if they hadn't moved on
their mating calls drowned
by the cries of onions

all summer long the garden littered the yard
these intricate literate vegetables were talking
with my mom she'd read at night at the table
file away in the fall in glass jars

come spring out she'd go
rain or shine &
there she'd be she'd
come back changed even in winter
they would not refuse their small
breathings, murmurings, rings
& rings of memories they turned
& tossed in their sleep

seeds shining, thinking of mother

when you leave me

will you
slip
under
breath

leave me
where you bend
near
sleep
or wake
will you, then
slip your
arm from

under my   breath
your breath   )

falling back
into

small garden
carbon dioxide has
bloomed & died in

under my breath
back   into when
you love me

& when you leave
will you still leave me
breathing will you
take my breath away

winnipeg in winter

                    iron lungs in the basement
                          blood lifting

              every room
        breathing through teeth

        lines rooms like wallpaper
        climbs the stairs

        cold in its mouth tumbles down

                                under the cold sky
                          winter a giant & sleeping body
                                  fitted with stars
                          we move slowly all winter in

                    moonlight sour as cider

        though we are patient, wait the season
        sounds it makes, alive
                  thoughts move in & out
        pass through skin & bones
            relieved to be out
                          to be in
        the skin we curtain our lives with

                    moves inside
            our lives
                  /short of air
                                the way we inhale
                                the way we inhale
                    one another
        the way we are made
                  \whole
                                almost
                  mad   we are
                        that   close

canadian love song

          cold as rock once
      moon has broken
the stem a storm at the wind
         ow a yell
         ow petal

    the flowers the pain of their
slow sudden life the birds bang
on a bitter & empty air they cry
       when theyre wrenched

their fractures lady   & some
              time when it is double
     jointed when it is

    warm your dark dark weight
your face & the moon
          thicken on desire
                sometimes
      your breath

        falls

              in freckles
   on my face

it's catching, my love

in the dog
days it's not
the pitch
the dog says
but the cat
ching i ching
the hot sun
the slight breeze i
ching you know
i ching you ching
we all ching
for ever
y thing
in chat or hat
we ching

let's face it we all are
aching for a little ching
here a ching there a ching
every thing is it ching

c'mon open yr eyes eh
someone's throwing up
poe ms fro mthet ips oft he fin ger
sknu ckleb all the ysay but
it's all heart the tall heart
's turbule

nce they drop

int($_0$

you waiting
your heart's a bun
dance not sure which way
they will go or which

way you your
self to go won

de ring wh ere it'sg one the air
ript off the 216

st it ches one for ever
y day the ypla yis it
that hold tog ether the figure-
eigh the art pulling ap
art the love
you lob aga in & aga in up tome
its wo bble i feel
helpless
you have me
in st itches
alm ost hope
less to get by

the cri sis in what it says its sur
prise when before it re
aches
you falls
out of pre
dest i nation fli psb ack & for th
as tutter
on it sway
to at
ten tion
then ewa iri tent ers
mo vesa
bru pt
ly do
W_N
or o
ver
OVER
or do
wn a con
tusi on in a ir

yr thots are
mu rmurs in the he art ru
mours you can no tcat ch
un lessy ou ha ve
a la rgeness it can

                              fall in un
                          less you move
                        wit hout kno wing
                      qui ckl yon you rown
            hear
                    t's in
        -dire ction
                      thest itches pul ling
                            whe rey oum ovew
                        heny our ece ive
              theth row in love with
                  thelo ud ing
                      -ing in you rears
                                        a pers on could come
                                          down with it
                                              it's cat
                                        ching you know
                                        i mys elf am cat
                                            ching on

    the presti dig it at i ont hat pre sses thro ugh
          st rike swith surpr isei tsar rival
                  thi sag it at ion th iss leight
            o fha nd wec all love

                                        second base
                                        lying there
                                    like an as pirin

              me wondering if
              i'm really going
              to catch it
              now

at night cooley listens

at night cooley listens to his body
an answering service he bends over now
        the day's over the day's messages
the rest of the day he does not listen
does not pay it much attention, his neglect shameful
cooley knows he shld do better shld take it out more often
        show it a little more affection

once the noise of day drops like shoes untied away
every night when the tired switch clicks night on
the body becomes importunate spouse
it's about time you listened to me
you self-centred bastard the body says you barely listen
the body rehearses a long list of grievances, sniffling
           && there are violins

cooley remembers his friend arnason the alarm
that clambers like small primates in his eyes his stories
death in subways beneath Leningrad on Strasbourg up
stairwells under Toronto clouds lounges lined
with mortality beside august in Gimli Arnason broods
on death on principle warms nests
crowded with death eggs he bills & coos under

        && now cooley too knows death
          will not leave him how
         ever unfaithful he'd be
            nor he her for
        death has wiggled her bum
            he can't resist

sometimes cooley's body tries to reason with him
        its sockfoot honesty

      listen it says you better
         smarten up cooley
       me im not gonna take this abuse
           any longer

I could go to the police you know ˙

cooley tries not to be too alarmed
   it belly-aches a lot, the body
      and lies
  it lies through its teeth
  especially when he's given it drink
    & late nights out
 the body comes home bitching & ungrateful

         he's learned that
        20 years of false alarms
        one terror after another
     the body engages in hit & run tactics

   sulky from neglect jealous of strayed attentions
      the body thinks cooley is interested
         in every body but his own

       when do i ever get any
   time with you the smallest bit of love cooley
   it's because I'm plain & a little unglamorous
    isn't it isn't it but whose fault is that
      you never spent a nickle on me
 & yr out big shot playin' around all smiles & charm
  you cheap bastard what's wrong with me huh
why yuh always oogling other bodies answer me that

    don't you love me no more i thot you loved me
)body switches tactics
     you said you did, once
      sd yd always be true
    & we had some good times
   we were young didn't we Cooley
  winces there was a time he was proud
    to be seen with his body
   dressed it in a tan & open shirts
  took it out to places & looked at it
   when it wasn't looking but now
 it looks back foggy-faced in the mirror

yeah cooley says, wary as a snake handler
what you got to tell me this time
leans over to look into the body's eyes
there must be truth there, bare
as a new polished car, hurtful to look at
painful as cooley's tongue all sores & slurry but
sees nothing, eyes droopy as marshmallows

        pain the body says I got pain
   there is a flute cooley hears faintly off stage
      real bad cooley i got it bad this time
                where where does it hurt
            Dr. Cooley says *are you sure*
           where is it what is it this time
   wonders is he being professional too solicitous
        is he being sucked in again by the body
           little prick, how it malingers & feints
               it sabotages every night out
     insists on tagging along in winces & preparations
stores up evidence all night for all-night recrimination

my side it's the kidney the body cries out
goddamn kidney's killing me do something
it's time you smartened up faced a few facts
your side my eye Cooley cries but his heart's not in it
thump thump Cooley's heart says, kettle drum
& then faster louder thumpthumpthump a snare
drum goddamn kidney again cooley thinks
leans over has learnt to float on the adrenalin
when it washes ashore, sweeps at his fate

his fear squirts like a carburetor in a formula-1 car
cooley hears death death cooley has cancer cataracts
catarrh has concern hears bassoon hears
oboe hears panic cooley is a man
whose kid has run into the street, not looking
thinks he must cancel his appointments
but can't he can't let people down death death
not though death croons in his lymph nodes
not though coronaries cruise his red seas like sharks

cool Cooley must be cool
as an undertaker must not
make a fool of himself
not over something like death
it can get under your skin
ring worm you aren't careful
it can break your heart yr not lookin'

so what yr always belly-achin'
every time I sit down yr at me
yap yap yap just get home
hard day's work & it's hypochondria city
cramp in the left calf sore throat speed in the heart
& yr sick all over, you can't help it
know what you are, yr a royal
pain in the ass is what you are

hurt hurt hurt says the body turns saxophone
right kidney says it can't hold on much longer
says pain says death says 12 strings says
I'm goin' down Cooley & I'm

takin' yuh with me you & yr abuse
thump thump Cooley quickens
it's spread the cancer's got him
by the balls thump thump ^{thump} Cooley knows

it's death in two weeks
4 days
one guy, perfect shape, went in Friday
died the same weekend
cooley angles for time needs time
has poems to write fantasies to fant

this isn't fair the kidney going out
the two-timin' kidney on a date
& no replacements it makes him
sick the way kidneys have no pride
show no loyalty & theirs a family business

listen are you sure Cooley says *you sure*
thinks of kicking the piss out of the kidney
                     its pulling his leg the asshole
bang bang yr dead the body says & there are cymbals
this is a symbol Cooley thinks
the body has things to tell him

why you always letting death come between us
huh answer me that cooley that's all you ever think
you come home at night we got a chance
could spend a little time together
& that's all you can think about
it's death this death that death said this
& not one word for me, not a word
why can't you get death off yr mind, she can't be that special
why can't you be true to me huh
i'm yr body ain't i we bin together a long time
we go back a long time you & me
why you doing this to me

                 at last cooley knows death
                 has fallen overboard cries
            out in the hot chambers of his heart

cooley & the body wrangle for hours
until at last they tire at last are tender
in the long late night could almost be
                 lovers, cooley & kidney
talking it over inmates of death

                     pain the body moans
                         death cooley wails
                 they could be into the blues
              cooley tearful the body might leave him

                 they try to make up once more
                 the two of them making sorrow
                         full music talking
                 it over, intimately, all night long

4

New Poems

winter dark

for months there would be rain & darkness
this was after harvest & the geese had gone
you would move through it houses would float on
water on the face of the earth this big shadow
horses in gumbo & yr gramma bundled up
to her neck in trouble & grumbles
pots stuck to tables & floors

& it would move it would move through you
long fields of darkness cold stalled in
shed just plunk right in there banked up to the knees
                      & freeze solid

a few of the places the allison place
a yard light would float into night
it would flood the ice and skate around
tug at winter until it would dissolve a patch

snow shone & christmas the fuzz of lights
skies so open stars would buzz where they hang
                    : thats winter
   & oranges   fat in our hands
                 fat with promise

                   all winter we moved on cold & dark
                   small boats on that clay
                   small bells we struck into blindness

willow island

cranes disappearing
the air dissolving

clouds breathing
on our face

frogs they say are dying
where they sing at the end
of cat-tails
green through the cold reeds
the panic spring

heron on the tip of the island
starched sky it stands upon
strange heroine
a dowager in waiting

piece of fog \
stuck on day

hangs from its patience
tugs at the strings it stands upon
& cannot move

bird drops shade like a high
rise apartment little
things think to find
rooms in

cranes into shale
caverns of wind
lift their slow
necks turn
into long slow kites

legs trailing
broken reeds behind

how crow brings spring in

or no not that actually
they are magicians in capes
whisk it in from under their arms
             crepes of sun

                        or egg

foo yung in black tights acrobats tightly wrapt
out they strut in those black shorts
             & march crashes
them onto a trampoline wet with lights

or lands them feet first
on the plank of spring

                  & at their feet
                        aahhh the canadians sigh
      green   tumbles up up
          onto the air over&over
              sommersaulting
            & everywhere   somewhere
                        it may be
      may maybe
          vaulting to summer

  under the big top
  in the spotlight
it runs & drips
        down the canvas

            our faces open as kids
        in gum & carmel
                        on a binge
                  stuck all over
  our eyes and our feet

            we are struck by
        we are stuck on
                        spring

           imp
    inges

               crow un
        hinges /spring

spring frogs

                         : frogs
                                 revolve
                 revel in frost
               their emerald brains
             the sharp stars
                         sting their eyes
                                 reveal

                 frogs
               stuck like rocks in mud
           the nightspring pinned to their skin
                         scan sky for
                             stars   & spin

                 when their brains line
               up on ganglia of stars
                           they sing back
                     up millions
           of tiny green trucks
                         dump
                 their gravel
                 ravelling with light
                           into the dark pools
                               the pin wheels of night

littoral, june

birds work edges of water
expectant as nurses
robins black birds grackles circle
the sprinkler shh sshh shH
they hop and wade
pants to their knees and baby
jays drink but do not douse
their stubby blue flames
new robins with measles
wash their small feet

bird-silent they
/ dip into mouths

pull their irridescence
in sweaters over their heads
later they will show
their young the small
voltage under their wings

gulls

they scraped
            their wings on air
    cried & cried
                long sounds
that sank in the lake her body was
            & never came back ever came
                back to her

    the narrows where birds lived
                    her mind swam
        rocks light wrecks on
she could feel the slop slop of its weight

now she pins spider legs
            round the wind
                        & the water
            lunges in & out

        the sun when it sets
                    in her heart
        is her heart
torn out of the sky

tidings

small boat floats
against the dock

its coat of slime
knocks the dark over

waters it arcs & bumps
makes sounds its tied on

& then the squall of muscle
the water the boat the tide

on its moorings
a roar & a row boat

trails its rope
on sand in the aftermath

whale a mass of red
meat & the boat

chinks by in sonar
sings its boat songs

its lesions on the shore

urban gothic
[*a*- without + *lyssa*, madness, rage]

they reach in reach down
ten ton tentacles dangle
under pavement they are

all the black & broken veins
dip bent fingers rip
open pipes & arteries

feed hungrily on summer
the hot green scream

elms turn into elegant & painted ladies
shriek with their finds the green
finery they deck themselves in
linger in the streets longer & longer
in their hot lingerie

all summer ears covered we listen & dream
wish for white asylums sweet alyssum
winter when our minds fill up with snow

spider plays the leading lady

spider stands on her bridge
speaks line after line into the dark
water we tread she threads her life through
threatening lines talks terrible lies
her come-hither hightop boots

& her socks [audience breathes
audibly] coming un
done falling off her
long long legs revealing
night & day we swim wondering
how she pulls it off

meanwhile spendthrift spider flaunts her wares
speeds up & down moonlight fluent in ecstasy
gathers charms on the lines she strums & flings

bright shiney things strings them
along draws them taut draws them
to our attention has every intention every
morning when we stoop
to inspect her twinkling
the small beads she tells
to the first light

spider teeters on a spiteful & goitered existence
does she ever wish when she unrolls her lingerie
the way she feels it in her fingers does she
in her hip ways ever think
she would like something more
lasting does she fear sometimes
late at night she will end up running
to fat macrameing all alone by moonlight
the moon itself which once hummed
with light turning now
into a spud in a muddy sky

variations on bees

                    among the ragweed
they could be ragpickers
they click like women at gambling
wheels when they open
hoods & doors in the yard
the parking lot fills up with them

dig in their heels &
          heave on pipewrenches
          bend over & ratchet

          colours & smells out
bees slouch on bent fenders open
          bottles & smoke

there at the end of the rain
          bow the pots of gold

beleagured ants tow off the wreckage
          eyes flashing day & night

                    *

bees those little hot dogs
hot shots in outrageous capes

hit the flowers spring
back nimble tumblers

when they land
doing sommer
saults & flexing

their stout little bodies
in tight flannel pyjamas
doing marathons on a tramp
oline sky trampling through the malathion
plastered with mustard

*

they took up lodgings
negotiated with june &

spent a lot of time in the sauna & sun
room sniffing pollen sipping tea

they adjusted their leggings
in sunwaxed rooms that glistened
                    they listed & listened

the roar when you bump
their terrible longings

*

bee drags its barbecued body over
sticky things socks round its ankles
            itch while the bee works
a yellow roll where they bulge
    its legs covered with coarse hairs

        the wet
    petals   /dont dare
        breathe   hold
                    their pale pastel
    breath
                as long as they can & longer
                    the bee panting & short
    of breath crawls
        its fatness over them

a series of shocking pre-positions
& after

                                    words

to place be

                    fore

                                              or in
                              front
        of:

        about   be low   from   to
        above   beneath   in   to ward
        after   beside   in side   through
        ahead   betwixt   off   through out
        around   between   on   under
        at   by   out   until
        a way   down   over   up
        back   during   past   with
        before   for   since   within
                behind

had we but word enuff:

                    to   before   in   of
                        place   or   front

                                                    & time

                    time &
        time again
                                this
                                    my lady
            would be

thats an oh oh

know what lorna said

lorna said the onion is
an O in an O in an O
thats what an onion is
(oh) thats what it is
thats what she said it is

but an O is an O is an O
dont she know
it comes before P
cock (OH) you dont say

but if she had kept her ears o
pen (OHOHOH) looklooklook
its a matter of ear
i told her myself
but she wouldnt listen
she would have seen (OH)
havent you heard

the onion   is not
(OH)
a series of Os (OH NO)
not even a (OH) wooden O
the pearl that is beyond
(OH YEAH)
these are pearls that were

no wonder the onion is (OH OH) crying
it should   be it should   bring tears
to your eyes   it is so thin
skinned
it makes   my mouth
water cant you see the on
ion is bawling its head off

OH - *OHHH* - *OOHH*

&（*OHHH*）i want it so

the onion   you can see （（（ ）））   is absent
        minded is having
    you on is getting it (oh no)/ yes
                    just ask me
                            //on
        or off ,, terra bulbous & utterly unen
                        cumbered unem
            barrassed about it
                pleased you might say to be so unem
        ployed the onion played that up a lot

                the onion is the pearl beyond
        serren   dip it ously sexy
                those hopped up little bulbs
        that turn on / turn you on on you (*OH!*)
                    in the middle of the night
            ))) you want
                                            /it

                    （*OH OH*） so bad
                        you ohhh can taste
                                    /it
                        startled little gonads
                        all in a row
                            o gogogo
                            go nads go

ohh such sights   & sounds & smells
    love living under
        ground driven under or into (parent
                thesis) onion is
        driven is driving me wild

a nut in the dirt
        it is an O-nut dough
nut there oh do not disturb
            the vowel which is beyond

all constancy, imagining: to pull an O out   of the ground
                    nothin left but grund
     you could get the dirt on the onion if you really tried

        oh onion
                        you should save it up all right   pack it in
                all night   you should
                    savour it is hot for it
                            for one wild (oOhHH) shaking
                    mouth to mouth

                            the Great Vowel
                        howls in your northern mouth

                        so how come
        lorna said that   the onion is an O
            (OH) how come
          she dont let the O's go
     off into the O-zone) where all things begin
                & where they came from
            where they can float in little umbrellas (practically

                nothing wld come of it but oh no
            she cant offer   ohh a little
          console ation say a few letters or two
     a consonance she could send us
     into ecstasy the O's can lean on
                        she could offer a beta O
                  pinion
                                & Lorna with
            holding her name
                        shame on her
                    ohohohoh
              she's getting crozier all the time
         bad mouthing the onion so
            you can hardly hear it
              how can she
     bear it   how can she keep it
                                /up

((o)) ((o)) (o) (o))))

        it is
)you can take it
from me(it is stuttered it is
   naked   with s(o)r
                      r(o)w

  full music
          ow ow ow

   how can she
   want it so

swept/

((a granary
              loud with wind
a wind heavy and old in its rafters
        a grey wind
                   small stones of wheat
   stored in the bin
and still the slow strange wind
                        rolls through and it
           razors
      the light
in spring dead smells
                         & rats
         running
               & then the
         swallows wet
                      dripping
         puddles of air
   outside
               the land
lasered with light
        fine green hairs
   the long slow wind